THE SCOTTISH IMMIGRANT

ISOBELL McCONNELL

Dedicated with love and affection
to my mother.

THE SCOTTISH IMMIGRANT
Copyright © **2019 Isobell McConnell**
All rights reserved.

ISBN: 978-0-9946174-5-3

Published by **Meredian Pictures & Words 2019**
Ballina, Australia
No parts of this publication may be reproduced, stored in a retrieval system, or transmitted in any form or by any means, electronic, mechanical, photocopying, recording, or otherwise, without the prior written permission of the copyright owner. This book is sold subject to the condition that it shall not, by way of trade or otherwise, be lent, resold, hired out, or otherwise circulated without the publisher's prior consent in any form of binding or cover other than that in which it is published and without a similar condition including this condition being imposed on the subsequent purchaser. Under no circumstances may any part of this book be photocopied for resale.
This is a work of fiction. On occasions reference is made to real events and people, and such references have been as accurate as possible. Any similarity between the fictional characters and situations within its pages and places or persons, living or dead, is unintentional and co-incidental.

Table of Contents

PROLOGUE 5

CHAPTER 1: Young Anne 8

CHAPTER 2: Young Jeannie 12

CHAPTER 3: Anne's First Child 16

CHAPTER 4: Alexander Macrae and Elizabeth 21

CHAPTER 5: The Cowells in Dunfermline 26

CHAPTER 6: Dysart - Alexander's Troubles 29

CHAPTER 7: Opportunity 42

CHAPTER 8: The Cowells' Early Days In Melbourne 47

CHAPTER 9: Migration 53

CHAPTER 10: Arrival 71

CHAPTER 11: A Moment Of Clarity 82

CHAPTER 12: Exploring Melbourne 86

CHAPTER 13: Sewing Again 91

CHAPTER 14: The Macraes Come To Melbourne 104

CHAPTER 15: Edward 111

CHAPTER 16: Four Years Later 118

CHAPTER 17: When Edward Met Elizabeth 124

CHAPTER 18: The Wedding 138

CHAPTER 19: Travelling North 147

CHAPTER 20: Arriving In Mackay 154

CHAPTER 21: A Home In The Canefields 159

CHAPTER 22: The First Child 169

CHAPTER 23: Memories Of Wales 179

CHAPTER 24: The Italian Connection 185

CHAPTER 25: The Depression 191

CHAPTER 26: Rats 197

CHAPTER 27: A Day At The Beach Has Consequences 203

CHAPTER 28: Elizabeth Goes South 210

CHAPTER 29: Three Months And More In Melbourne 220

CHAPTER 30: Unexpected News, Twice Over 230

CHAPTER 31: Living With Isobell 241

CHAPTER 32: No More! 246

CHAPTER 33: Edward Returns To Melbourne 251

CHAPTER 34: Oakleigh 264

CHAPTER 35: The War Years 274

CHAPTER 36: Losing Tom 283

CHAPTER 37: Rosebud 286

EPILOGUE 295

ACKNOWLEDGEMENTS 299

PROLOGUE

What makes a person want to migrate? To sever, perhaps forever, the strings that bind someone to parents, home and country?

Elizabeth Macrae had long since ceased to ask herself this question. This desperate urge to break away from her family had been with her since she was ten years old. For as long as she could remember she had seen her mother Anne living in fear. Every one of those frequent times that she heard the sound of the coalmine whistle Anne dreaded that it would be her husband Alexander who was being brought up terribly injured or dead. There were hundreds of accidents in the coalmines around Dunfermline and along the Firth of Forth. Elizabeth's father was working in one of those very mines.

Elizabeth had heard her father speaking to her mother about the terrible conditions. She heard how the miners had to crawl along the narrow tunnels digging out the coal. How they struggled for long hours breathing in the foul air, with coal dust coating their lungs, causing them to cough up black phlegm.

There were rotting timbers supporting the tunnels in many places and rock falls were frequent. Elizabeth had been with her mother in 1910 when her neighbour's husband was killed in a rock fall. She stood with her mother at the funeral and saw the devastation on the faces of the family as the miners lowered his coffin into the ground. Without his mining wages, the family would be forced to move and Elizabeth wondered how they would manage. There were four young children left without a father, and now without his pay to support them.

Her brother Robert was born in 1906 and it was obvious that like most of the sons of miners, he would end up joining his father in the coal pits where there were plenty of jobs for unskilled workers.

The births of Fay in 1908 and Janet in 1910 locked the Macrae family into permanent poverty, and further disillusioned Alexander, who faced the reality of never owning his own cottage. In frequent moments of unhappy reflection he realised that it meant that coal mining was to be his livelihood until the end of his working days.

Life for Elizabeth did not improve when her family was forced to move the 14 miles to Dysart in 1918 after the closure of the coal pit in Dunfermline.

The slagheap in front of the coalmine towered over their new home in Dysart. Its looming dark presence dominated the village. The coal dust blackened the tenements, and seeped into the miners' lungs, the pores of their skin and all their clothing. Accidents happened often in the mine pit as there were few safety regulations and only primitive technology. The unionization by the mineworkers was beginning to help to reduce accidents, but it was still a dangerous occupation. In Dysart there was no other choice of work for most of the men. Hard as it was, Alexander loved the comradeship he shared with his workers, and he at least knew that he had the security of permanent employment.

The need for coal was urgent with the outbreak of The Great War, and thousands of men were employed coalmining along the coastline of the Firth of Forth. That changed after the War. By 1918 there had been many closures of mines around Fife, although the mine at Dysart was, as yet, still profitable for the colliery owners.

This mine extended out under the Firth of Forth itself, and the miners had to face the dangers of rock falls, or of pumps failing as they worked deep underground.

Each week Elizabeth witnessed Anne's efforts just to feed all the family. Each day she watched her mother struggle to cope and to survive. It was no wonder that Elizabeth dreamt of escaping to a new world. A world where the air was fresh and clean, and the sun shone. A world where fear had vanished.

.oOo.

CHAPTER 1: Young Anne

Anne Jamieson, who would later become Anne Macrae, was born and raised in Lanark. Her father John was a coal miner. His wife Isobella had endured four miscarriages before Anne was born in 1871. Their daughter was to be their only child.

When Anne was five the Jamieson family moved to Dunfermline, where they lived in a 'but and ben'. Sometimes these houses were called 'two up and two down'. Two families shared each house. A 'but and ben' was constructed of grey stone with a front door opening from the street onto a central passage that ran through the middle of the building. Each family's home consisted of two rooms: a main room on the ground floor with its entry opening off the central passage, and an upstairs bedroom. The two families shared the toilet in the small yard at the back, the water pump and a washhouse.

John was determined that young Anne could attend the new Junior School in Dunfermline. He knew the importance of education, and hoped to be able to keep her at school for as long as possible.

It had been in 1872 that Scotland moved to State sponsored free schools and education became compulsory from five to thirteen years, and the new school was built in Dunfermline. It had been decreed by the education authorities 'that poverty was no excuse to stop attendance'.

Anne and her best friend Jeannie felt lucky to have the formal education unavailable to many of the previous generation. They met on their first day of school in 1877.

In their teens the two girls then moved across to the 'higher' grade school in their district and they both hoped to succeed in eventually passing the 'Leaving Certificate Examination'. But John's meagre wage meant it was impossible to keep Anne at school when she turned fourteen, as fees were charged to attend the 'higher school' from that age, and it was impossible for her parents to pay them. Young Anne was deeply saddened when she was forced to quit her classes. However much Anne's mother Isobella and her husband John dearly wanted their daughter to continue on at 'higher school' with her friend Jeannie, they could not find a way to make that happen.

"We canna afford the fees Anne, and we need you to get a position in Dunfermline to help us," explained Isobella, as she looked into the shock and despair in Anne's eyes. "Your father has spoken to his supervisor and he knows of a family that needs a domestic in their home."

Anne's eyes filled with tears at the thought of leaving school, and losing any chance of ever following her best friend to St Andrews University. The University was famous throughout Scotland. It had been established in the early 15th Century and was acknowledged for its academic excellence throughout the United Kingdom. It was a dream that would now never be fulfilled.

Jeannie was also devastated at the thought of not sharing the excitement of continuing her education with her dearest companion. On Anne's last day at school, Jeannie hugged her friend.

"I will always stay your friend, Anne. You must promise to visit me at home and we will share stories of our lives always."

Jeannie thrived at 'higher school' as she loved learning and expanding her knowledge. Her Aunt Mary encouraged Jeannie to tell her about her days at school and was filled with pride as her niece excelled each year with her studies. Jeannie felt very fortunate to have such a caring aunt who made sure that she had plenty of time to study. Together they often visited the Public Library that was funded by the philanthropist Andrew Carnegie.

Carnegie's benevolence contributed much to the best memories of Anne's childhood, as it did for many more young Scots.

Andrew Carnegie was born in Dunfermline in a weaver's cottage in 1835 and he started work as a bobbin boy in a textile mill at thirteen. It was the decline of hand-loom weaving that had forced the family to emigrate to America in 1848, but he never forgot his birthplace. In 1855 the family moved to Pittsburgh, USA, and it was from here that he made his fortune.

Carnegie became a wealthy industrialist who over the years, speculated in shares in railways, and eventually become involved in locomotive construction, bridge building and other investments. Later he controlled a huge Pittsburgh based iron and steel business.

Although he made his home in America, Andrew Carnegie always maintained an enduring love of his birthplace. With the wealth of the USA quadrupling in the later half of the nineteenth century and the vast expansion of the railways, 'Carnegie Steel' made Andrew one of the richest men in America. Even from his home in the US, he was a great benefactor of Dunfermline. He made remarkable gifts to his beloved native town, including the large Public Library and the Public Baths in town.

It was Andrew's father William in 1808 who had helped to found Dunfermline's Tradesman's Library, and Andrew never forgot his father's legacy. He built upon it by providing over 2000 libraries 'for the masses' in Scotland.

Anne loved visiting the library and the baths and knew she was blessed to live in Andrew Carnegie's birthplace. She kept visiting the Public Library as often as she could, borrowing the novels that Jeannie had studied at school. The two girls had many long conversations discussing the themes and plots of the novels as well as sharing secrets with each other.

Dunfermline was indeed very fortunate to have Andrew Carnegie as a benefactor. He and his wife Louise holidayed frequently in Scotland, purchasing a large Highland Estate in 1897 in Sutherland. He gave many rich gifts to his beloved birth city – a place he once described as 'the most sacred spot to me on Earth'. His gifts included the historic Pittencreiff Estate, given to the city for a public park in 1903. He said it was "to bring into the lives of the toiling masses of Dunfermline more of sweetness and light."

Pittencreiff Park was where Anne and Jeannie often met on Sundays. It had become the place that provided a welcome escape for many of the miners' families in Dunfermline as they wandered through the magnificent Estate near the city.

The girls' lives would take very different paths after their parting at school. But that friendship, sustained in the park and beyond, would remain strong, and those paths would intertwine across the years to come.

.o0o.

CHAPTER 2: Young Jeannie

Moira McGregor had died giving birth to Jeannie in a miner's tiny cottage in Dunfermline in 1872. Jeannie's father Bruce had watched, terrified, as the blood poured between his young wife's legs while he held the newborn baby in his arms. The midwife had looked on in horror as the cord broke away from the placenta.

"My God, there's nought we can do! It's only the hospital may save her, but we canna move her, and even if we could, how can we get Moira there in time?" cried Bruce as he thrust Jeannie into the midwife's arms.

The bairn was still covered in blood, wrapped in the soft piece of white cloth, with her tiny arms flailing in the air as she was handed over.

Jeannie was giving out loud cries that seemed to fill the air with the terror that Bruce felt as he bent over his beautiful Moira. His tears flowed down his tired lined face as Moira briefly opened her eyes and lifted her arms to close around Bruce's neck.

Moira's labour had commenced twenty-four hours ago, and as the contractions strengthened and the intervals between them shortened, the young mother-to-be felt that something was dreadfully wrong. The pain simply and totally consumed her, and no matter how much she was forced to push, the cervix did not seem to want to stretch to allow the agony to end.

Between bursts of pain the question rang inside her head - "Och, why did I not get the midwife earlier?"

This was Moira's first child and she had supposed that the baby was not due until three weeks later. Bruce had finished his shift at the mine twelve hours earlier and once aware of his wife's difficulties he had raced out of their home to bring the midwife to try to help.

With the last of her remaining strength, Moira had pushed till she was sure her heart would surely just give up, and then bliss! The head and shoulders appeared.

Dimly Moira heard the midwife's voice express her alarm. Then she felt the warmth of Bruce's body as he reached down to lift her body into his arms. The sound of the baby's cries gave Moira a wondrous sense of peace. She could sense that there was no doubt that all was well with their new bairn.

Bruce looked into Moira's blue grey eyes and sobbed, "We've a braw wee lassie, and I am so proud of you."

Moira's eyes closed as she died peacefully in Bruce's arms. Bruce vowed that he would do all that he could to make sure Jeannie had all the opportunities he had not. He swore that she would succeed in her education and break away from the poverty that he was sure had helped lead to the death of his Moira.

Moira's sister Mary lived nearby and Bruce put Jeannie into her care. It was not long after Jeannie's birth, when Mary moved into the cottage with her brother-in-law to care for both of them. He was devastated by the death of his wife Moira, but Mary helped Bruce cope with the loss as she became the mother to Jeannie and adored her as her own.

The grief Mary suffered at loss of her sister was lessened as she watched her niece grow. There was comfort in seeing the likeness to her sister in Jeannie.

Bruce loved his sister-in-law and he knew he could never have coped without Mary's love and care for his daughter. His life was also made easier and more bearable by her becoming his housekeeper.

He always looked forward to finishing his mining shift and returning to his home to be met with such warmth and love from his sister-in-law and his daughter. There was always a good tasty meal, hot water, laughter and conversation with Mary and Jeannie. As Jeannie developed her reading skills with her increasing education, she read to Bruce often, and he delighted in sharing and listening to her stories.

Jeannie's ambition at school was to pass the entrance exam to St. Andrews University, and her father Bruce and her Aunt Mary did all they could to help her. Jeannie passed her 'Leaving Certificate' to the great delight of her father and aunt, as she was the first child from a miner's family in the district to achieve such a level in her education. Jeannie was Bruce's only child and he had been determined to see his daughter finish 'higher school', and to keep the promise he made at her birth.

He had hoped that she would attend St Andrews University in Edinburgh where women were now admitted and could graduate in in the Arts. It had been a struggle for Bruce to find the school fees each year and often he worked extra shifts in the mine to make sure he could pay them.

St. Andrews University changed the course of Jeannie's life, as that was where she met John Cowell, who was studying medicine. Jeannie had turned nineteen and John was in the second year of his course. They married when John finished his third year of study. Jeannie and John went back to live in Dunfermline in the Cowell's family home where John started his medical practice after completing his degree.

The Cowells were to play an important part in the lives of both Anne and her oldest daughter Elizabeth, in a place far from the coalmines of Scotland.

.oOo.

CHAPTER 3: Anne's First Child

Anne was fourteen when she left school but she and Jeannie remained close. Anne was now working long tiring hours as a domestic in a large, wealthy home in Dunfermline, but the girls kept up their friendship. Often they would meet at weekends at the wonderful Public Library, or in Pittencrieff Park. Anne enjoyed visiting Jeannie's home as often as she could and was always made welcome, as Mary understood how important their friendship had become to both of them.

When Anne started working it became difficult to maintain such a close friendship. Anne's hours were long and exhausting as she worked in the kitchen helping the cook, and cleaned out the fireplaces every day. She also helped out in the laundry: constantly heating the heavy cast iron, ironing and folding the linen, making sure it was not scorched.

The job had come about when Anne's father had made inquires at the mine and was informed that the mine manager Mr McNeill needed a new housemaid. John approached the manager who arranged for Anne to meet his wife. She was impressed with Anne's cleanliness, intelligence and appearance. The girl started at the 'big house' the following week and for the next four years proved to be an excellent domestic worker.

Andrew McNeill was the oldest son in the family. Over the years Andrew had observed Anne growing into an attractive young woman. By the time he was nineteen he was over six feet tall, lean and powerfully built and studying at St. Andrew's University.

One day while home visiting his parents, Andrew was in his room when

Anne knocked on his door. Andrew called out for her to come in. Anne intended to clean the hearth. Andrew walked over to Anne and said, "What a bonnie lassie you have become."

He pulled her across to his bed and pushed her down. The young man lay over the top of her and as he placed his hand over her mouth he smiled and said, "Well, this is a good surprise before breakfast!"

He was still in his nightshirt as he thrust one hand between her thighs and pulled down her pants. "Well young lassie, I bet this is what you have been wanting!"

Anne felt a sharp pain as he thrust himself into her body, and she thought she would be torn apart. She tried to twist away but it was impossible as he held her arms above her head and the weight of his body pushed her down into the bed.

She was still a virgin. She and her friend Jeannie had always agreed that they would wait till they eventually married before 'losing their honour'. Like most young women of the time, they feared an unwanted pregnancy and the shame that they would feel. The grief it would bring to their families also terrified them.

Andrew finally pushed himself away and said, "Dinna you ever speak of this! No' that anyone will believe a skivvie who worked here with this family anyway."

With horror Anne looked down as she tidied herself, and saw the blood seeping between her thighs. She cowered at the side of the bed sobbing, and vowed that she would never tell what had happened. Mr McNeill was her father's boss and she was terrified that her father would lose his job.

Anne knew too that the McNeill family also had their reputation to uphold in Dunfermline and would never allow a scandal like that to be passed around – there would be no question as to where the 'blame' would lie.

How could she even tell her own parents? Illegitimacy was regarded as such a sin in their strict Protestant home. In many such homes, single mothers were regarded as 'fallen' women who had sinned against the Church and were treated with disdain and disgust at allowing themselves to succumb to their 'lust'. Little concern seemed to be given to the circumstances of the child's conception.

John and Isobella were shocked when Anne did finally have to tell them. She was now five months into her pregnancy and it was impossible to disguise it. Anne sobbed into her mother's arms as she told her of her trouble.

"I canna tell you the father's name. Please never ask as I will never reveal who he is."

John and Isobella Jamieson loved their daughter deeply. She was their only child. Isobella was horrified when Anne later quietly told her of the rape. She blamed her husband and herself for forcing Anne to work as a domestic at that home. However Isobella was frightened of what John would do if he ever found out about the shocking rape, and the two women promised they would keep it a secret from him.

Anne felt so ashamed and humiliated that she even vowed not to see her friend Jeannie again. She thought to herself, 'I canna go tae her, carrying this illegitimate bairn. She would nae want tae be seen with me. How could I explain tae her what had happened?'

Over and again in her despair she asked herself, "Was it ma fault?" for all that she knew in her heart that it hadn't been.

Anne also knew that if she lost her position in the McNeill household her family who needed her wage would suffer. Often Anne bought home extra food from the kitchen of the home. She managed to keep working there till she was almost seven months pregnant, never revealing the truth. Anne knew that she would not be believed if she said that the older son Andrew had forced himself on her.

When Anne's daughter Isobell was born, her parents knew that she would always be a part of their family and Isobella claimed her as her daughter. It was a Scottish tradition to always give the first granddaughter the grandmother's name.

"Aye, Anne we'll care for our granddaughter as if she is our ain. We love her and she is part of our family," Isobella reassured her. "Dinna worry, we will treat her as if she is our ain daughter."

Her parents were as good as their word. Soon after Isobell's birth Anne had a chance to work in the linen factory in Dunfermline and train as a weaver, where she would have the opportunity to gain a skill.

Anne carried the burden of her shame for a long time. Isobell was almost seven years old before she finally contacted Jeannie again, and that was only after the birth of her second daughter Elizabeth. Anne was now twenty-six, and she vowed that Jeannie would never know about the circumstances of her first daughter Isobell's birth.

.o0o.

CHAPTER 4: Alexander Macrae and Elizabeth

John Jamieson worked in the mine with his friend Alexander Macrae. He visited John and Isobella's home occasionally, and often walked with John to the mine.

Anne was into the final three months of her pregnancy and she was frightened for her future and for her unborn baby's life ahead. She knew how illegitimate children and their mothers were often treated with scorn, and that many lived in great poverty in the mining villages.

Alexander found himself attracted to Anne's shyness. He greatly admired her long black hair, which she tied into a plait hanging past her shoulders. Her soft round blue eyes, white skin and the gradual swelling of her belly stirred in him a desire he had not felt for years.

John had spoken to Alexander about Anne and the imminent birth of their first grandchild.

"We will always love Anne but I don't know how we will manage with another bairn in the household," John admitted to his friend.

"If Anne will consent to marry me, I will be proud to care for your bonnie lass and her baby. I'll be a guid father to the wee bairn and I've grown very fond of Anne," Alexander replied.

The soon-to-be grandfather appreciated the offer, and gave his blessing to the proposal. Anne trusted Alexander and she knew that she and her child would be safe in his care, and have their own home.

When Alexander asked Anne to marry him, she looked into his face and sobbed, "I'll be a good wife to you, and always care for you."

Alexander was thirty-seven, considerably older than his new bride. In her heart Anne knew that she was not yet in love with her husband, but she was determined to make their marriage work.

The newlyweds moved into a rented miner's cottage in Dunfermline after their marriage, and Alexander became the only father Anne's daughter Isobell ever knew.

Anne had been proud of her new 'but and ben' although she looked forward to a time when they would have a place of their own that they wouldn't have to share. Alexander promised that they would get their own cottage in a few years.

Alexander was a loving father to his stepdaughter Isobell - he was highly respected and well known in Dunfermline. However he struggled to earn enough to grant Anne's wish to own their own cottage. Gradually he came to hate the living conditions in the small rented tenement. The slate floor in the main room was laid over earth and was damp and poorly ventilated. Pools of stagnant water lay in the yard most of the year, spreading out from the washhouse, and Anne was constantly worried about the affect the dampness had on their health.

In his frustration, Alexander thought about his cousin Douglas. Back in 1865 Douglas had been only nineteen when he migrated to Vancouver. From there he had headed out to the Canadian wilderness following the Frazer River into the heart of the Rockies. Alexander was ten at the time his cousin left, but over the years his parents often spoke of the many letters Douglas wrote to his family telling them of the fortune he had made prospecting for gold.

Douglas had joined up with a Canadian prospector and they had managed to find several large nuggets in the alluvial streams. Alexander had started working in the coal mine at twenty, and he had often thought of his cousin's success in Canada but he did not have the fare to get there. It was not until he had the responsibility of caring for his Anne and Isobell that he decided he would take the chance and leave for Canada. However he was now in his late thirties.

Optimistically Alexander believed he would have the same luck as had Douglas and told himself that after a few years, 'My wee family will never have to depend on the coal mines again for their livelihood.' He thought, 'I'll earn enough money through prospecting to send for my family and set up a new life far away from the poverty we all have struggled with, working for a pittance in the mines.' He was desperate never to work as a coal miner again.

It was a year and a half after he married Anne, when Alexander left for Vancouver. However by the time Alexander arrived in Vancouver and he commenced working along the Frazer River, coping with the harsh conditions, there was little chance of finding gold.

Thousands of prospectors had arrived before him, and the gold bearing alluvial sands of the Frazer were already depleted. His cousin Douglas who was now 49 had long left the Frazer River area and set himself up as a trader somewhere in British Columbia. He was becoming very wealthy selling goods and spirits to the prospectors.

Anne's dream of a better life in Canada disintegrated upon Alexander's return. After a wasted year on the Frazer, he had been forced to work as a labourer around Vancouver's wharves for another three years, with no hope of earning his fare back to Scotland. It led to Alexander drinking in the taverns at night, searching for any company and attempting to blot out the pain at being parted from his Anne and her daughter Isobell.

At last Alexander managed to work his fare back to Scotland on a steam ship. He then managed to get his old job back as a coal miner working in one of the mines near Dunfermline. He had suffered much hardship in being forced to stay in Canada for four years.

Elizabeth was born exactly nine months after Alexander's return in 1904.

Her father was delighted, saying, "What a braw wee bairn she is. We'll call this wee-un Elizabeth. This lassie will no work as a skivvie for anyone. I'll make sure we give her a good trade." He said to Anne, "I promise you, lassie that one day we will own our ain home. We will live away from the mining towns and our children will get many more opportunities than we have had."

He loved Elizabeth dearly as she was Anne's gift to him after the misery he endured in Canada.

Anne had come to love Alexander, and she believed in him. He worked so hard but she wondered how his promise could ever be kept. He was unskilled and untrained for any trade, fit only for labouring and mining, with his physical strength his only asset.

While Alexander was in Canada Anne had found work again as a weaver in Dunfermline. She had moved back into her parents' cottage and her mother Isobella cared for her granddaughter while Anne worked long hours weaving in the large linen factory.

Those years in Dunfermline were, in some ways at least, good ones, as the Public Library and the gardens of Carnegie's Estate in the city allowed Anne to indulge in her love of reading as well as enjoying some wonderful walks.

After Elizabeth's birth, Anne had renewed her friendship with her dear friend Jeannie. Isobell was now six and had started her schooling. Anne walked to the Cowell household where Jeannie lived with her husband John. They hugged each other and their seven years separation faded into the distance as Anne was welcomed into the Cowell household, carrying her beautiful dark haired baby Elizabeth.

.o0o.

CHAPTER 5: The Cowells in Dunfermline

Young Elizabeth became very attached to Doctor Cowell and his wife Jeannie in Dunfermline. She had visited them since she was a tiny baby and the Cowells loved Elizabeth as their own daughter. Anne's friendship with Jeannie became very important because she continued to visit the Cowell household almost every week. Doctor John Cowell spent as much time as he could spare with Elizabeth whenever Anne visited and he grew very attached to the girl. He had observed Elizabeth develop from a tiny baby.

As a small child Elizabeth would put her arms out to be picked up by John, and he would lift her high into the air as she chuckled and smiled at him.

He often remarked to Anne, "What a bonnie lass we have come to visit us today."

Jeannie remained childless after several miscarriages. John's affection for Elizabeth showed in his delight at her weekly visits. He also knew that it meant much to his wife Jeannie to have Anne as a close friend.

Anne trusted the Cowells and many times allowed her daughter to stay overnight with them. With the birth of more children: Robert, and later Fay and Janet, Anne's life became much more demanding and Elizabeth was often given permission to visit the Cowell family by herself.

Over the next few years Jeannie and Anne's laughter filled Elizabeth's young ears as the two women recounted their experiences as young girls and teenagers. Never a week passed without some new titbit of information that was overheard by Elizabeth, either from Doctor John Cowell, or by listening in on her mother's conversations with Jeannie.

John Cowell had hoped to start a family soon after their marriage but after three miscarriages John's friend (a specialist in women's health), advised him that it would be dangerous to Jeannie's health to try to conceive a child again.

Doctor John had met Elizabeth soon after her birth and it was little wonder he became very attached to her. He thought of Elizabeth as a blessing to their lives and her regular presence helped to ease their sadness at being a childless couple, with Anne's weekly visits to their home. Elizabeth was bright and intelligent, eager to read and to learn.

By the age of ten, she was reading some of John Cowell's medical books and she had many surprisingly frank conversations with John Cowell, who was prepared to give much of his free time in answering the many questions that tumbled forth from her lips.

Elizabeth possessed a pale milky white complexion, with just the lightest blush of pale pink on her cheeks. Her hair was a mass of black curls. She had round hazel eyes that shone with intelligence, and which were highlighted by long dark lashes. The girl's warm generous smile whenever she was in the Doctor's presence meant he always found the time to find a few precious minutes away from his busy practice to welcome the wee lassie into their home.

All her life Elizabeth would remember how Doctor Cowell used to swing her up into his arms and crush her into his chest saying, "Welcome little black haired Bess, and what do ye want to discover today?"

As Elizabeth developed and became much more self conscious about her awkward gangliness, her rough cotton dresses and torn stockings, the greetings were not as spontaneous. However the friendship and closeness Elizabeth felt towards the Doctor was always there when they were together discussing medical terms they came across in some of the journals that she was allowed to browse through.

It was devastating for fourteen-year-old Elizabeth when the Dunfermline pit was closed and her family was forced to move to Dysart. She could no longer visit the Cowells. So many of their conversations had centred on life in the city, and on the library books that Elizabeth was able to borrow from the Carnegie Library, or the wide range of classical novels that Elizabeth borrowed from the Cowell family.

Occasionally young Elizabeth would be allowed into the surgery to explore the wonders of Doctor John's 'special room'. The large jar of sweets beckoned from his desk and could never be resisted. To hear a heartbeat pounding into her ears from his stethoscope, and to occasionally glance at some of the medical diagrams in his books, were treats never forgotten.

.o0o.

CHAPTER 6: Dysart - Alexander's Troubles

As it was, Alexander's wage barely provided for enough food and rent, but it was his drinking that caused greater poverty and with it, fear and tension most evenings. A move of fourteen miles – a long journey then when transport could be difficult and expensive - from Dunfermline to Dysart had not helped. Over the years he had become bitter about the lack of safety and poor working conditions at the mines including the mine owners' treatment of their workers. Their shifts were long and the pay was poor.

By 1924 Alexander had become pit manager and he was responsible for checking out the safety of part of the mine. His son Robert, now aged sixteen, had also started work at Dysart's Lady Blanche mine. The miners called it the Dubby mine. Alexander was deeply saddened to see his son Robert following him into the mines. He was not disappointed in his son, but the circumstances of their lives. Seeing Robert working at the job he himself had come to hate only added to his bitterness and distress.

Every time the whistle sounded at the end of the mine shift, Elizabeth would watch her mother's face tighten as she waited for Robert's entry into the room. Robert had started work at the Lady Blanche pit in 1922. He had pleaded with his mother and father to start work, as there was a close bond among the miners. The boy wanted to be part of it and to join his father, working with him. There was almost no other work but the mines, and in truth they needed the money, so Anne reluctantly agreed. With great misgivings and sadness she had watched Robert stride down the road with his father on his first day of work.

Elizabeth would place a boiler of water on the hearth each day, in readiness for her father and brother to appear after the long day's shift. Their faces were black with coal dust, and their miner's clothes thick and blackened. Alexander and Robert would strip their clothing off, and wash the grime from their faces and hands. (At sixteen, Robert hated undressing in front of his sisters as he stood in front of the hearth!) Anne would then lift the clothes and take them to the outhouse at the back of the cottage where the resident families shared the two troughs.

Following her mother as she carried the filthy clothes, Elizabeth would carry out the boiler of water and pour its contents into the trough. Often some of the other wives shared the trough and added their heated water also.

'Och I wonder whether they'll stop for a wee dram tonight?' the girl sometimes mused to herself as she waited for the water to boil. If there was a bar open at the end of a shift it was usual for some of the miners to stop and slake their thirst on the way home.

Unfortunately Alexander seldom stopped for just the one 'wee dram'. Too many times Elizabeth would sit on the small bed in the alcove, trying to concentrate on reading and attempting to block the shouting and abuse that Alexander would hurl at Anne so often after his drinking bouts.

Later he'd try to explain. "Annie, I canna do without the drink as it washes the coal dirt out of my throat. Sometimes we are on our hands and knees crawling along the tunnel two miles out into the Forth. I widna wish it on any animal, and I wid give my life to have been able to keep Robert out of the pit."

Alexander's face was the colour of a deep grey sky. There were rings of deeper grey under his eyes and he had a sharp hacking cough that welled up from the depth of his lungs. Often he would be doubled over clutching at his stomach as waves of coughing consumed him. He had worked in the mines now for over twenty years and his lungs were filled with the black dust.

No wonder Elizabeth dreaded the sound of her father's footsteps in the passage. The verbal abuse, the striking of his hand across her mother's face when he found the stew not hot enough, or the flavour lacking because there was not the money to buy enough decent meat – all were memories that would always haunt Elizabeth.

"Och ye canna make guid gravy out o' chucky stones, young Bess," said Anne, "but your father will never understand that wi' his drinking."

Anne had given birth to Robert when Elizabeth was two. At six years of age Elizabeth had to spend many hours after school caring for him, walking with her mother helping push her brother around the parks of Dunfermline. But Robert was a joy for the family and Elizabeth loved him so deeply that she never felt resentment toward her dear little brother who now took up so much of Anne's time.

Alexander had been overjoyed at the birth of his son and just as he'd wanted only the best for his daughters, he promised himself that Robert would have a future that was not tied to any coalmine in Scotland. But in Dysart there was no other future for the sons of miners except the hated coalmines.

There was never any hope of even saving enough to buy a small cottage.

Anne longed for some peace and a chance to quietly shut herself away and read like her daughter.

Before Anne's marriage to Alexander she had often visited the Carnegie Library in Dunfermline. It was a dream to one day be able to visit there again and lose herself in many of the amazing books that she could access. Anne missed those visits to the Cowell's home. In six years of living in Dysart Anne only visited Dunfermline four times.

There was little chance of any peace with their two rooms now crowded with the children. Even outside those rooms they were too often cheek by jowl with the Rawlstons - the other family that shared the 'but and ben'. The Rawlstons were not bad neighbours, but their closeness only added to the general noise and busy-ness of life.

Anne and Elizabeth could no longer turn to the Cowells for comfort. In 1918, the same year that the Macrae family had moved to Dysart, the doctor and his wife had migrated to Australia. Although Jeannie wrote to Anne at least twice a year they were very conscious of the distance that was now between them.

The Macrae home was in a part of Dysart called the Braes. Alexander and Anne had hoped they would only have to survive the 'but and ben' at Dysart for a short time but their stay there had stretched to six years. It was now an unspoken fact that this would always be their home as long as Alexander worked at the mine.

Elizabeth vowed that one day she would leave her impoverished home. She believed there must be something better to call home - better than the permanently damp floor, the open coal fired cast iron cooking range and the cramped bedroom she had shared with her young sisters, Fay and Janet.

Isobell, Anne's oldest daughter, had married a man named Callum McCallum and stayed in Dunfermline, but when the mine there closed they also shifted to Dysart. He too worked at the Dubby mine, on the same shifts as Alexander.

The McCallums also rented a 'but and ben' in the Braes. It gave Anne much pleasure to visit her oldest daughter and share the local gossip with her.

There were several coalmines in the area, and over the years accidents had caused the deaths of many local coal miners. Often when that happened families were evicted from their homes with very little payment given by the owners of the mines. That cold-hearted response caused great suffering to the surviving wives and their children.

Even many years later it was still so very vivid - that bitter cold Tuesday in 1924, the day of the accident. It was exactly a month earlier that Elizabeth had turned nineteen.

When she was fourteen, soon after they had moved away from Dunfermline, Alexander had managed to get her an apprenticeship in dressmaking in Dysart. The dressmaker, Mrs McKenna, was pleased to teach Elizabeth the skills of cutting, sewing, beading, and tailoring. Elizabeth had proved to be an excellent learner. After four years of her apprenticeship, Elizabeth was now highly skilled, and she was valued in Dysart for her dressmaking ability. The young woman also brought much extra business to Mrs McKenna.

Elizabeth sewed dresses for her sister Isobell and her mother Anne, and made jackets and suits for her father and brother. Her father was very proud of Elizabeth's skills.

He often spoke to his fellow miners and said, "No daughter of mine will become a skivvie for any family. My Bess will now always be able to earn her own money."

It was early in the afternoon on that cold fateful Tuesday, and Elizabeth was beading the bodice of a dress that had to be finished at the weekend. She taken the work home and was bent low over the black beading, her eyes peering at the fine work. She was finding it difficult to concentrate on the dark fabric.

"I dinna ken what we'll have on the table tonight," said her mother. Then Anne had a thought, and said, "Elizabeth, take this threepence to the wharf and pick up a nice piece of cod."

Anne knew Robert enjoyed cod, and it also had the advantage of being a very cheap meal as she had little left to spend on food after Alexander had spent it on the drink.

Elizabeth clasped the threepence tightly in her hand and smiled at her mother as she said, "It will be good to get out into the fresh air of the harbour. I'll talk to my friend Willie McClay. He is sure to give us plenty of cod or haddock and I saw him heading down the Braes early this morning on his way to the dock. Willie had looked across at our window and I waved to him."

Willie's father Douglas McClay worked at the pit with Alexander and they were usually on the same shifts. Willie had spent most of his days at the docks since he left school. Even before then many days were spent there when the lad should have been at classes. As soon as he turned fourteen, he was offered a job as a deck hand on one of the fishing boats. His family considered themselves lucky, as it meant there was no shortage of fish on their table. Willie was one of the few sons of Dysart not to be taken to work in the coal pit. Life in the mine for fourteen-year-old boys was a thing dreaded by nearly every coal miner, and their sons.

As well as a mining town Dysart was also a port, and it had once depended on the sea for much of its early prosperity. It did still possess a quaint harbour that dated from the early years of the seventh century. Before coal became the main export, salt manufacture was a very flourishing industry in Dysart for many centuries. Salt was used to preserve fish, which was once one of Scotland's main exports.

The old saltpans had been on the flat ground near the harbour and there was plenty of coal in Dysart to boil the seawater. The industry at one time gave Dysart the nickname Salt Burgh.

The breakwater stretched out from the harbour and sheltered the fishing boats of the Firth of Forth fishermen. Elizabeth loved walking down the cobbled road to the harbour, passing the town square, the Dysart post office, and St. Serf's church with its old 80-foot high tower.

She passed the Bay Horse Inn. It was built in the 16th Century for the son of Lord Sinclair, the Earl of Rosslyn. Elizabeth looked up and observed carved bear heads on three corners of the inn. She had learnt they were thought to represent King James V1, his Queen and their son. The inn once served the sailors who came into Dysart harbour, and the carters who brought the coal to the harbour. Now it was where her father Alexander spent many nights drinking, causing so much misery for her mother Anne.

Elizabeth walked passed Pan Ha where stone cottages now stood instead of the saltpans, and then out onto the breakwater. The waves lashed at the base of the old slipway where shipbuilding had once been a thriving industry in Dysart.

The harbour was now a ghost of what it once was, as the larger ships took much longer to load their cargo and the business was lost to the larger ports of Mehil and Burntisland.

Elizabeth looked out and counted five fishing vessels in the harbour and two small ships, as well as a few coal ships. Some of the small ships that came to Dysart were bringing in clay for the local potteries. Others brought wines and spirits.

Looking back at the village, breathing in the salty air, watching the waves crashing against the breakwater, and observing a fishing boat bobbing frantically against the waves as it entered the harbour she could almost put out of her mind for a while, the poverty of the miners. The poverty, and the mine itself that continued to destroy so many lives over the years.

Willie was standing on the breakwater. He called out to Elizabeth, "Well if it isn't young Bess come to visit me. Ye might be looking for a guid piece of cod. We had a guid catch today."

Willie was now twenty and Elizabeth was the lass who had taken his heart.

When the Macrae family moved to Dysart in 1918, Elizabeth was fourteen and Willie was fifteen. Their fathers both worked at the Lady Blanche pit and Willie used to meet her at church where the families both went on Sundays. Now nineteen, Elizabeth was beautiful with her dark Cowelly hair, soft creamy skin, well-rounded breasts and a slim waist. She also had wonderful curved legs and slim ankles. Alas for Willie she had refused his many requests take her out.

At the breakwater Elizabeth was smiling. "Mother will be pleased and the cod will be good and fresh. It is Father's favourite meal," she said happily.

Willie looked into Elizabeth's eyes. "Ye are such a braw lassie. What about coming out with me this Sunday?"

"Och, William, I've too much dressmaking to finish. I've a wedding dress to bead. Maybe another time."

Elizabeth was fond of Willie and his cheerful banter. But when she arrived in the port town at the age of fourteen she had promised herself that she would never marry a Dysart lad, and that one day she would leave the place forever.

"Just a wee kiss on the cheek will do for now," said Willie as he handed over the parcel of cod. "Maybe another weekend."

The young beauty smiled and said, "Ye are a cheeky lad William." She leant forward as Willie lightly kissed her cheek, and then continued, "I'll need to get back to Mother, as Father's supper needs to be ready when he comes back from the shift."

As Elizabeth walked past the post office she heard the loud mine whistle. It was only just gone 2pm and she knew that it was not the end of a mine shift. Elizabeth knew immediately that something had happened at the mine. She felt the tightness in her chest and realised that her mother Anne would be very anxious too.

She quickened her steps as she turned into the Braes, where her family lived. The short sharp pierce of the mine whistle echoed throughout the small village and all the inhabitants, whose lives were completely governed by the mine, knew what grim news it probably carried.

On that Tuesday afternoon when they heard the whistle, Elizabeth's home was filled with a tense chill silence, just for a few seconds. Anne had been knitting a dark brown cap for Robert. Her hands gripped the knitting needles tightly, causing her knuckles to glisten white against the wool as she said to herself, "Och, it is probably just a wee cave in."

Anne had lived with the threat of the whistle sounding out its warning for twenty years. Its noise still frightened her just as it had when her Alexander first entered those black grimy pits and she had learnt the terrible significance of that dreaded sound.

It was less than a month ago that the whistle had pierced though the town on a cold bleak afternoon. A cable had snapped, dropping the cage down over 100 feet, killing two of the miners who lived at the Braes. The wives were still in shock and the Braes tenants were still coping with the loss of their friends.

Now that her only son was also working at the Lady Blanche pit alongside his father, it doubled Anne's anxiety.

In his job as a 'pit manager' Alexander was required to go ahead of his team and inspect the roofing, checking out the wooden beams and sometimes crawling into small spaces in the tunnel, looking for any likely mine collapse. Although the job carried danger this made Alexander highly respected by his team.

Anne was seated near the stove working at her knitting as the shrill whistle sounded. Elizabeth had just walked through the front door and into the downstairs room as Anne looked up at her.

"Dinna worry mother, that whistle often sounds for just a minor accident," she said, trying to be reassuring.

It was half an hour after the blast of the whistle when Robert entered the room. His tall lithe frame seemed stooped and shrunken and the coal dust clung to every pore of his exposed face and body. His blue eyes were red and swollen. His tear stained face had a grotesque, almost mask-like appearance where the young man had rubbed at his eyes, leaving big greyish circles around them.

Anne looked up and was shocked at the look on her son's face.

Robert entered with his brother-in-law Callum stepping into the room behind him. The tears and sobs tore through his chest as he spoke, "We couldna do anything. Father walked into the pit - Callum and I were following him and we were only about fifteen yards behind him."

"We heard him shout and we found him pinned to the ground by a stone weighing about twenty- five hundredweight, which had broken into three parts. We managed to get him out from under it, but Father died on the way to the surface. We were so close to him, but nobody saw the thing happen."

Robert's sobbing had almost stopped but his chest was heaving in and out, trying to catch his breath as he said, "He's dead, Mother. Father is dead."

Callum, Isobell's husband, walked over and hugged Anne. He said, "I think that Alexander had been tapping the roof with his pick, checking the supports, when it fell on top of him. It happened at the start of the shift. We were only a few yards away. When we heard him shout, Robert and I rushed to his aid and found him lying unconscious with the stone on top of him."

Callum stepped away from his mother-in-law as she her bent over with her face in her hands.

"He was lying face down, the stone having struck him in the head and back. He was severely injured on the face and ribs, and one of his legs was broken. I think it would have happened so fast he'd have felt nothing. We drew him out, but he expired on the way to the pit head without regaining consciousness," explained Callum.

Robert then spoke through his sobs, "I was side couping a hutch when I heard Father's shout. Just after the cry I heard something falling and rushed to see what had happened." After a pause he added, "I think the stone must have broken before it fell. It was about 8 feet long, 4 feet broad, and fifteen inches thick. They are working at slate rock now and it is very seldom that type of rock breaks. Father must have been putting in a pillar as we had been warned about the stone. The foreman warned us before he went in."

The young man caught his breath again before he continued, "Father was a very brave man as he probably saved other men's lives by checking out that rock."

Although previously Alexander had never been hurt very seriously, he had had a lot of accidents and had some very narrow escapes. His job as the mine inspector came with many risks as it was his role to check for loose stones and to carefully check out the pillars supporting the rock.

Elizabeth could do nothing but walk across and hug her mother. Anne sobbed into her daughter's chest, "We've lost a guid father and I dinna ken what we will do without him. He loved his family and he suffered greatly because of his work in that mine. He hated it and now he is gone."

.o0o.

CHAPTER 7: Opportunity

Three years had passed since the death of Elizabeth's father and she was still working for Mrs McKenna. But now she was a fully qualified tailoress with good dressmaking skills as well, and was receiving over three pounds a week. Often the clients were so impressed with the expert tailoring and dressmaking that they gave Elizabeth extra money.

The seams on the dresses, beading and buttonholing on men's jackets and suits were tailored to perfection, but working in low lighting was affecting Elizabeth's eyes and she was concerned about a future working such long hours as a tailoress.

Mrs McKenna often remarked, "Aye, Elizabeth was such an accomplished dressmaker that one could turn her work inside out and no-one would notice."

Robert was now twenty and his body was hard, lean and well muscled. He had thick curly brown hair, an engaging wide smile and did not have any problems meeting the local lassies. He often came home very early on Sunday morning after spending his time dancing with the lasses, but he had no favourite.

He was determined to make his mother's life easier, helping her with his money and providing extra small luxuries such as the occasional bottle of whisky. Anne often remarked, "Och aye, a wee dram of whisky in the evening is God's liquid," although she never came to depend on it as Alexander had done.

The other miners at the pit respected Robert as he hauled as much as most of the men. He was proud of his work, and like the other experienced miners he thought of himself as one of the elite. Working at the coalface you had to be strong and tough. When he was not working at the mine on the weekends, he played football with the Dysart mining team, or he went dancing on Saturdays. Sometimes he would walk long distances to another mining village for a change of scenery, and a change of company.

Robert often remembered the days when he would get out of the cage and head the short distance home with his father who always asked, "How do you like the experience Robert?"

The son always answered, "I like it well, Father." He did not wish to let the older man know that he was nervous and even afraid when he occasionally saw some of the large pieces of slate rock falling into the mine tunnels.

With the passing of the years Robert became indifferent to the many dangers of the mine. If someone was killed he would be worried for a few days but then concern about the incident would pass. He did not talk about it to his mother.

By the time Robert was twenty-two, he was drawing one hundred hutches a day. The hutches were the small coal wagons that ran on rails. Each was filled with coal before the men had to push the loaded wagons to the cage. They were then raised to the surface with a winch. He took risks to get the coal out but the money was good compared to other unskilled labourers.

Robert did not think much about the future. He just lived from day to day and looked forward to the weekends. Unlike his sister Elizabeth he did not see a future beyond Dysart, and he enjoyed the company of the miners. He had no other skills but coal mining, and he did not have any desire to leave home, as his mother needed him.

Anne had received a funeral grant from the Coal Board and a small pension from the local miners' Permanent Relief Society after the death of Alexander, but it was a pittance. With Robert now receiving a full miner's pay of over six pounds a week and with Elizabeth's help, their household was just keeping above poverty.

However the threat of eviction was always there as the mining company owned their home, and gradually the mine was producing less coal and becoming uneconomical. Elizabeth still held her dream of migration and many times muttered to herself in both longing and frustration, as she observed the blackened faces and exhausted bodies of the miners trudging along the road after their shifts.

She said to herself many times, "Bonnie Scotland? Ah never ken what is so bonnie about it."

"There goes Queen Bess, she's aye thinking she is too guid for the likes of us," Elizabeth would catch some women saying within her hearing as she walked along the dingy street to her house after a long day hand sewing, or bending over the Singer treadle sewing machine.

Elizabeth's chance came in 1927 when she spotted a small article in the Dunfermline newspaper. She had saved over one hundred pounds but it was not enough to chance leaving Dysart without some support.

With the passing of a new law: *The Empire Settlement Act of 1922*, the

British Government agreed to lend up to three million pounds a year for fifteen years to the Dominions to "promote Empire settlement, and re-distribute the white population of the empire whose prosperity would thus be increased." Elizabeth read that, "following an agreement about passage fares, a thirty million pound Agreement was made between Great Britain and the Australian Commonwealth."

The two Governments were also to lend 34 million pounds to the Australian States for a period of ten years for approved schemes of development. In return the States in Australia guaranteed to settle an assisted immigrant for every seventy-five pounds received.

From Jeannie's letters to her mother Elizabeth knew that Doctor John Cowell and his wife had settled in Melbourne.

Elizabeth was inspired and excited by the article she had read. "Mother, please write to the Cowells and ask if they would sponsor me to Australia as their domestic, and I will do dressmaking for Jeannie and her friends as well."

Five months had passed before Anne received a letter from the Cowells agreeing to sponsor Elizabeth. The paperwork was ready and was enthusiastically submitted. Because of her qualifications and sponsorship by the Cowells, she was to sail on the *Beltana* out of the London docks in December 1927 at a cost of ten pounds. A subsidy was paid by the Government, and the balance by the Cowells as her sponsors.

The authorities in Australia hoped that with the Agreement signed by the Commonwealth and the British Government, many of the 'New Australians' would settle on the land. But most of the migrants, like the Cowells, came from British cities and it was in the cities of Australia such as Perth, Adelaide, Sydney or Melbourne where they intended to make their mark.

.oOo.

CHAPTER 8: The Cowells' Early Days In Melbourne

The Cowells had settled in a rambling house in South Yarra near Melbourne in September 1918. It was a Victorian design with a central passage that had large rooms off either side.

The embossed ceilings were twelve feet high, with large windows letting in plenty of light. There were four large bedrooms, each with a fireplace surrounded by beautiful tiling embossed with flowers. The two front rooms of the house were extra large; one was the drawing room and the other was intended as a generous dining area suitable for a dining table seating twelve. The large tiled bathroom had a cast iron bath, with a pink granite slab cut around a white basin stand and a freestanding sewered toilet. The kitchen and scullery were at the back of the house opening onto a wide veranda. At one end of the wide veranda was the laundry and at the other end of it was another toilet.

The block on which the house stood was half an acre, and there were several gum trees at the front of the building that shaded the wide bull nosed veranda. Wrought iron latticework topped the veranda, and the heavy wooden front oak door had two panels on either side of it with brightly coloured red, green and yellow lead light designed in a long geometrical pattern.

John knew it would be a perfect house for his medical practice as one of the front rooms was so large that it could easily be converted into two rooms comprising the waiting room and his surgery.

Another entrance was constructed at the side of the home leading directly into the waiting room and Doctor John was finally able to open his surgery in February 1919. In the four months before John could commence his practice the late November weather suddenly turned from temperate to hot as the northerly winds floated down from the scorching plains, raising the temperature into the low nineties for several days in a row.

They had left Dunfermline at the end of winter in early April with the snow still on the hillsides, and slush and mud in the streets. The icy chill of the arctic winds bit into the skin, and the thick smog of the coal fires intruded into John's lungs causing him to cough violently at times. The doctor knew that as much as he suffered, the conditions were even more seriously affecting the lives of many of his mining patients. For John Cowell, Melbourne was a marvellous place to settle.

The hot north winds provided a sensuous experience as the warm beads of perspiration trickled down his back and his thighs. To wake in the morning with a soft cotton sheet across his body, and to feel the warmth of the breeze at such an early hour was paradise. John never wanted to see snow again.

However for Jeannie these new experiences only increased her homesickness and longing to return to Scotland. She hated the swirling dust of the north winds, and the huge garden surrounding the house with all its native plants made her feel isolated from any contact with neighbours.

She longed to be back in Dunfermline where she had status, and friends like Anne and her daughter Elizabeth, who had been such a big part of her life. Jeannie missed the feel of the city with its great cathedral, parks, and huge Carnegie library – she missed the sense of belonging to it all.

It was only eight months since leaving Scotland and Jeannie kept her thoughts to herself, hoping that she would eventually begin to adjust to this new environment as she already realised John would never return. Jeannie did not venture outside into the garden often. She worried about the harsh sunlight, which made her arms turn pink, and her face grow red with the heat. She had lost weight as she felt ill with homesickness for Scotland, but it was difficult to let John know of her unhappiness.

The surgery had been open for a few months and the large brass plate at the front gate announcing *Doctor John Cowell M.D.* was already attracting a growing number of regular patients from the area. Suddenly there was an outbreak of Spanish influenza in Melbourne at the end of 1918, brought about by men returning from Europe at the end of the War. John was very worried that he would encounter among his patients some that had contracted the deadly disease. It was extremely virulent as it attacked young healthy adults with amazing speed, "overwhelming the body's natural defences, causing uncontrollable haemorrhaging that filled the lungs resulting in the victim drowning in his or her own body fluids," as the medical books described it.

John had learnt of the spread of the influenza pandemic in Europe and the shocking number of deaths - numbers in the millions, and he was frightened for his patients and for Jeannie.

However the Victorian Government established a hospital for infected patients in Melbourne, with separate wards for males and females. Jeannie was shocked to see so many people wearing masks as they shopped. John insisted that Jeannie wear a mask and he implemented a program inoculating his patients. He set up the local treatment centre in South Yarra.

John told his wife of some of his women patients who were now widows left with young families. Schools and theatres were closed, and pubic transport was restricted. When a member of a family became infected, the house was isolated and strict quarantine rules were enforced.

By the end of 1919 the terrible disease began to abate. John knew that probably over a thousand people had died leaving many families in poverty. It left Jeannie resentful at leaving Dunfermline, even though the influenza epidemic was much more serious in the British Isles.

John tried hard to persuade Jeannie that their move to Melbourne would be very successful, but the first year was so traumatic for her with the threat of the Spanish influenza epidemic constantly on her mind that she failed to see the advantages of their new home.

Away from his work John got great pleasure from enjoying his garden. He loved the scent of the gums with their bright red flowers attracting many strange birds to the garden. He sat out on the veranda after surgery and watched the honeyeaters darting through the trees. The rainbow coloured parrots with their bright crimson, blue, green, yellow and orange feathers filled him with wonder as they dived in and out among the gums, and gathered in clusters letting out their harsh sounds as they searched for nectar. John knew he would never tire of his new home in Melbourne.

Sometimes the tabby cat from next door would glide along the top of the fence and leap down to crouch beneath the branches of the small wattle attempting to catch one particular pair of honeyeaters unawares. But the male bird always managed to dart away and often the smaller female, which John recognised easily because of her soft pale yellow chest, attacked the cat.

Often a kookaburra sat in one of the branches uttering that peculiar sound which always made John want to laugh with joy.

Dr. Cowell was now forty-five and his soft dark, thick hair had turned grey. The Melbourne climate was changing John's complexion from grey to a brownish pink glow. His eyebrows were now dark grey but they highlighted the blueness of his eyes. His Scottish accent would never alter and his patients found their new doctor to be full of warmth and compassion. Many enjoyed hearing a voice from Britain, as so many Australians were first generation stock from there, or new immigrants who were still proud to be called English or Scottish.

John found that for most of his patients, the attachment to Britain was still very strong. It was just over six years ago when Britain called on Australians to volunteer for the armed forces, and many of his patients who had left Britain before the war were among the first to enlist.

In fact for the first few months of the Great War there were many more volunteers than were accepted, but that changed as the war dragged on and the terrible loss of volunteer lives became known in Australia.

He was saddened to hear of the tragedy of two of his patients, Katie and her little daughter Judith. Katie and her husband James had migrated out from London in 1913, as it was their chance to find some sort of security with a job. However James had struggled to find work as he had no trade, although he had some experience as a labourer on the London docks. Katie was four months pregnant when James decided to enlist in 1915.

He had said to Katie, "Things are really tough in Melbourne and it's getting worse. At least I'll get four shillings booked to me every day that I am serving. It looks as if the war will last a while yet so you'll get regular money and if I'm lucky it will set us up for after it's over."

James could never have foreseen that he would end up a part of the sad ANZAC legend like so many of his fellow immigrants. A sniper shot him one day at Gallipoli, and Judith was born one month after James was killed.

John saw many such widows with their children - women whose husbands had died during the war. He always gave them time to talk about their problems, and their struggle to manage on the pittance of a war pension that they were given.

Sometimes young husbands came with their wives and it saddened him to see how many had amputated limbs, struggling with their crutches as they coped with a missing lower leg or foot. Regular work for those men was almost impossible.

By 1927 John's surgery was filled with patients most days, as he was highly respected and compassionate. He made sure that he took the time to listen to his patients, allowing them time to talk about their medical problems and their worries. Often the war widows just required a sympathetic ear. They discussed with the doctor the struggles that they had to cope with. He always treated the children of the war widows without charge, and the women for a very small fee.

.oOo.

CHAPTER 9: Migration

In 1927 the Cowells were able to finally complete the process of 'nominating' Elizabeth as the Agreement between governments required. As her "sponsors" they agreed to take responsibility for her accommodation and employment as a domestic in their household.

Jeannie was pleased at the prospect of having Elizabeth stay in their home, as she was a link to her friend Anne, and John had carried precious memories of Elizabeth as a child visiting them in Dunfermline. They looked forward to meeting her at the docks in Melbourne.

Elizabeth's passage was booked on the *Beltana*, which was a migrant ship carrying about 600 passengers. It sailed from Tilbury docks in London to Adelaide, Melbourne and then on to New Zealand.

Departing Scotland by rail to reach London, Elizabeth crossed Edinburgh's Forth Bridge, passing over the same body of water that her father and brother had risked their lives mining beneath, miles away. As she looked back at the misty shores across the Firth of Forth she was filled with sadness at leaving her mother Anne, her brother Robert, and her sisters behind in Dysart.

'I dinna ken whether I'll see them again. How will I manage without their love?' she thought.

Elizabeth vowed to herself that as soon as possible she would do all she could to get her family away from the poverty of Dysart, and try to convince Robert to join them also. She had dreaded the times when the mine whistle would signal an accident, with the possibility of a severe injury or even the death of her brother in the mine.

The train was called *The Flying Scotsman*, travelling via the East Coast Main Line. Elizabeth had never seen such a magnificent train; so impressive with the gigantic engine at the front with its steam bellowing out along the platform. She boarded the train and walked along the corridors between the carriages in a kind of wonder, passing a dining car, and discovering that her cabin was even heated!

The journey was to take about nine hours, arriving at London King's Cross. Her mother had packed some sandwiches but Elizabeth decided that experiencing the dining room on this marvellous train was not to be missed.

The soon-to-be emigrant arrived at Tilbury Docks by London taxi as her suitcase was large and very heavy. She was too nervous to attempt the trip by public transport - King's Cross Station was overwhelming, with people hurrying out of the station connecting to other trains. She spotted the taxi rank and gratefully gave directions to the Docks.

Elizabeth was greeted by a sailor at the entrance to the gangway, dressed smartly in his blue uniform and wearing his white cap with the name *Beltana* written across its band.

He easily lifted the suitcase onto his shoulders and said, "Welcome aboard! Your cabin number, miss?"

The cabin number had been printed on her passenger ticket. It was a relief to follow the sailor down through the stairwells and walk along the passage way to her temporary home. As he opened the door for her she was immediately impressed by the layout of the 'second class' cabin.

She had been allocated this because she was designated an assisted migrant, her fare being paid jointly by the Commonwealth migrant scheme and her sponsors.

Elizabeth was relieved to see that although the cabin contained four bunk beds there was room for comfortable seats, a wardrobe, and a mirror above the basin stand. In a cabinet below the basin there was a chamber pot.

There was also a porthole as the cabin was above the water line. Elizabeth had read that accommodation for assisted passengers had considerably improved from the early 1920s. Ship owners had upgraded, and built new vessels to compete with each other for the lucrative migrant schemes offered by the British government and the Commonwealth to convey passengers to Australia.

Recalling his own journey to Canada, Elizabeth's father had told her about the shocking conditions for steerage passengers on ships to America up to the early 1900s.

He'd described passengers crowded below decks with no privacy, appalling sanitary conditions, and food served out of pails.

However new regulations in force meant that 'steerage' was now actually second or third class. First class was quite luxurious, especially as high standards had been set since the building of ships such as the *Titanic* and the *Mauritania*. Sea voyages now were very popular with the middle and wealthy classes who were journeying to Europe and America. But all ship companies were keen to attract all classes by providing good accommodation on board their vessels.

There were two large drawers under each of the bottom bunks and Elizabeth was allocated one such bunk. The single deep drawer was quite large and easily held all the contents of her suitcase.

Her cabin companions were also assisted migrants and they too were aged in their mid twenties. One was a Scottish lass from Glasgow, and the other two women were from London. The two English women were disembarking at Adelaide.

Elizabeth was grateful to share the cabin with the young women and thought, 'I'll manage the long journey much better with their companionship.' She hoped that they would all become friends. She looked forward to meeting them later that evening when they were due to embark and commence the long journey that would take about seven weeks.

The ship was to sail early the following morning. Elizabeth had plenty of time to unpack her case into the roomy lower drawer underneath her bunk. About an hour later the cabin door opened and three women entered, followed by two sailors carrying their suitcases.

"Hello, I'm Sheila and my friend here is Jill," said one of the English women.

Maureen then introduced herself and Elizabeth was pleased to hear a Scottish accent again.

"Och, tis guid to be on board after such a long trip from Edinburgh - I canna wait to have a guid meal and a nice rest afterwards!" exclaimed the Glasgow girl.

Sheila and Jill were from the London area and greeted Elizabeth with wide friendly smiles. Sheila had a strong Cockney accent. They were both in their mid-twenties; slim with blond hair and wearing bright lipstick, modern dresses, cloche hats and heavy makeup.

Jill looked at Elizabeth and said, "Sheila and I have been friends since we were at school. We're looking forward to leaving the smog of London, and heading to Adelaide. We've been sponsored out as domestics."

Elizabeth was pleased to share her journey with these three women and was hopeful that they would all try and get on with each other for the next six weeks. Maureen was in her early thirties, with a plump figure, dark hair, round face, and a warm smile. She arrived at the cabin wearing a dark brown drop-waisted dress with just a smudge of lipstick.

Maureen was allocated the lower bunk and the two Londoners did not object to the upper bunk beds. These were easy to climb into with the stairs situated at the end of the bunk, and a half rail on the top bunks with white towels draped over them. There were snowy sheets and pillows with downy blankets folded at the end of the bunks. The cabin's porthole was large and above the waterline so it let plenty of light in.

'How different it seems to the conditions suffered by steerage passengers thirty years ago,' Elizabeth thought. She had remembered the stories her father Alexander had told of his trip to Canada in steerage all those years ago.

The four women found that the toilets, showers and two baths, were located along their passage and were spotlessly clean. They were not sure how many passengers had been allocated these facilities but Sheila said, "We'll work out the best times to come here. With only two baths available that could mean a queue though."

The dining room was spacious with long tables and comfortable wooden chairs. There were a few smaller tables seating six, which meant families could sit together.

Very polite and friendly stewards served the evening meal. It was tasty, good quality fare with generous serves. Fresh fruit was also available. The four women were impressed as it was much better quality than they were used to in their homes. Fruit was indeed a luxury for all of them.

The next morning Elizabeth awoke to the muffled sound of the steam engines throbbing quietly below her. The four women dressed and found that there were only six ladies sharing use of the bathroom and toilet area.

The breakfast was self-service with porridge, cereal, toast, eggs, bacon, jams and canned fruit available. The steward looked at the four women seated at the end of one of the long tables. He was handsome with dark Cowelly hair. He came across and chatted with Sheila and Jill whilst collecting the crockery and cutlery.

They flirted mildly with the man, as they were keen to make sure that he would notice them and maybe meet socially during the voyage. Elizabeth was aware how confident and worldly they seemed compared to her. She would never have openly encouraged him to flirt with her.

For the first three days the sea was calm and she enjoyed walking along the promenade deck, observing the people playing deck quoits and shuffleboard. The deck games were popular and she looked forward to joining in with a group. The lounge area had a small library with tables seating four, as well as an open space that was used in the evenings for dancing. Tea and coffee was set out on one of the buffets.

Waking early on the fourth day Elizabeth felt nauseous, as the pitching and rolling of the ship had increased dramatically. As she lifted her head a wave of dizziness overcame her and she felt like vomiting.

She groaned, "I canna go to breakfast - I feel so sick."

Maureen looked across from her bunk and said, "It will pass. You are just sea sick, but it must feel awful."

By midday Elizabeth's nausea increased and she had a violent headache. As she tried to stand, her stomach seemed to turn upside down. Her skin felt clammy with perspiration. She barely had time to open the cabinet below the sink, pull out the chamber pot and retch into it.

'Oh dear, I have never felt like this before. I think I could die,' she worried to herself.

Maureen entered the cabin, and was shocked at seeing at Elizabeth's deathly pale face. "I'll go and get the doctor and see if he will come to the cabin to see you."

Elizabeth replied, "Thank you. I couldna' manage to get up to the deck as I feel so weak, and I canna stand up without falling over."

About an hour later the doctor entered the cabin with Maureen. He had grey hair and was wearing glasses. He was neatly dressed in a grey suit and looked about fifty years old.

He felt her head, checked her pulse and said, "Well lass, you are suffering from motion sickness. I have many passengers who feel the same as you. There is not a great deal I can do for you but you must keep up your liquids. A sugar drink just sipped frequently will help, and I will give you something to settle your stomach."

Elizabeth was totally miserable and she could not bear to think of eating anything at all. Maureen kept her friend supplied with lemonade and water, but it was embarrassing to retch up into the chamber pot in front of her cabin mates.

Sheila and Jill managed to stay away from the cabin for most of the day but Maureen tended to Elizabeth, helping her to the toilets, watching over her whilst she showered and then helping her back to the cabin.

"I canna thank you enough Maureen. I hope we can keep in touch when we arrive in Australia. You are a wonderful, kind friend and we have only known each other such a short time."

"Well if one Scottish lass canna help another one what is the world coming to? My mother was very ill with tuberculosis and I nursed her for three years before she died, so a few days to help you is nae trouble at all."

Sadly the new friends lost touch with each other in the years to come, as so often happens with relationships formed in such transient circumstances. As good as intentions are, the busy-ness of life frequently gets in the way. In the days when 'instant' electronic communication was all but undreamed of, it was difficult to find the time for the effort required to keep in touch with someone not seen regularly.

It was three days before Elizabeth was able to leave the cabin and head to the dining room for breakfast. She felt totally drained of energy, but the awful symptoms of her seasickness had almost gone.

Later that morning she walked slowly along the deck and leaned over the side of the rails. The weather was fine once again with clear blue skies, and hopefully she could now get on and enjoy shipboard life.

It was a week before Elizabeth felt strong enough to join in with Maureen, Sheila and Jill to play some deck games. She enjoyed shuffleboard as it was simple to play and it gave her the chance to meet some of the passengers.

Sheila and Jill had no difficulty in searching out and finding some male company, as they were slim and attractive. Both had blond curled hair, and were using plenty of eye makeup, their eyebrows neatly plucked and highlighted, and using very bright lipstick. They could easily have passed as sisters.

Elizabeth noticed that they had plenty of confidence in conversing with strangers, and were experts at flirting. She liked the two women but was very conscious of her own appearance when she was with them. She never wore makeup except for some light pink lipstick. However, she had a smooth, pale cream complexion, a small perfectly shaped nose, full lips, with deep hazel eyes and black hair. She was also blessed with very slim hips, and shapely legs and ankles. The miner's daughter seemed unaware that she did not need any other attributes to be noticed.

One day Sheila and Jill were walking along the deck promenade, each one with their arms around two young men.

Sheila waved to Elizabeth and said, "Come and join us tonight in the lounge. Tom here has a friend he would like you to meet. You might like to try some dancing."

With some reluctance Elizabeth met the women after supper and was introduced to Tom's friend Richard.

The young man stepped forward and lightly shook her hand saying, "Well - this is the beautiful Scottish lass the girls have been telling me about. I would like a dance with you."

Elizabeth shyly responded, "Well, I'm no much of a dancer, but yes, I'm willing to try."

Richard was a paying passenger en route to Adelaide. He had an educated English accent and Elizabeth was impressed with his appearance. His hair was dark brown, was well cut, and combed to one side. He was wearing a tweed suit with perfectly fitted sleeves, and it was obvious to her trained eye that it was tailor made to fit him. He had soft full lips, hazel eyes, smooth olive complexion and a broad wide smile.

A steward set up records to provide the music and a dance waltz was playing. Richard held out his hand to Elizabeth and said, "Lass, this is our turn to dance."

Richard placed his arms lightly around Elizabeth and it was obvious that he was an expert dancer. He smiled down at her and she did feel a slight flutter in her stomach. He gave her confidence and it had been a long time since she had been held like this. She was surprised at how easy it was to follow his lead on the dance floor and she felt very relaxed, gaining confidence each time they danced together.

The evening went quickly with plenty of banter and laughter. It was the first time since joining the ship that Elizabeth had socialized in the evening with men and her cabin friends.

Over the next week Elizabeth spent part of each day with Richard. He told her that he had been manager of a men's wear shop in London specializing in tailored suits.

"I'm going to join my friend in Adelaide. He has established a menswear business in the city and we hope to open another branch there in a year or so," he explained.

"No wonder your jackets and suits are so well cut. I trained as a tailoress and dressmaker in Scotland and I ken well what a well cut suit looks like on a man," she replied.

After a week of seeing Richard every day, Elizabeth was beginning to wonder whether she was beginning to fall in love with him. He was so considerate and well mannered.

She loved the closeness of his body when he put his arm around her as they walked along the deck. She felt warm and protected. Yes, it did give her a tingling sensation in her stomach, and this felt so new to her.

Like many girls of her generation who'd grown up in a strict conservative environment, Elizabeth had clear and quite set ideas about what she expected and wanted in a marriage - a woman's only real gateway to security and social acceptibility.

Women who were still single in their late twenties and beyond were regarded with distrust by many. Not burned as witches like generations before, but life was certainly not easy. Banks would not lend money to an unmarried woman without a male relative standing as guarantor.

Attitudes were shifting, and there were now more girls like the two Londoners who took a more casual, even adventurous approach to life, but especially outside the big cities the old ways still held sway. Caution and conservatism ruled. Consciously or not, young women like Elizabeth had a 'checklist' of desirable attributes in a man.

Would he be a good father? (Children were of course inevitable!) Would he be a good provider? Did he have a profession, or at least a trade? Was he at least polite? If the man was attractive, well, that was a pleasant bonus. As Elizabeth considered this man she'd just met, he seemed to meet those requirements. Perhaps she could make a future in a new country with this charming man.

Richard spoke softly into her ear as they wandered along one day, and said, "Shall we meet again tonight? I am so looking forward to us dancing together again."

Without hesitation Elizabeth looked into Richard's eyes and said, "Aye, and so am I. You have taught me to waltz so well and it gives me so much pleasure to dance with you."

Unfortunately, the friendship with Richard that Elizabeth had hoped might grow into something more, came to an abrupt end late in that night. Elizabeth lay on her bunk bed sobbing into her pillow thinking to herself, 'How could I have let it happen?'

Richard and Elizabeth had walked along the promenade deck after enjoying the last dance, which was a romantic waltz. It was eight days since they had first met. The deck had been in darkness except for the glow from the full moon filtering its soft light onto it.

Richard turned towards Elizabeth and placed his hands onto her breasts, stroking them through the soft crepe fabric. She was aware of a hardening of her nipples, felt aroused by his touch and felt a fluttering feeling deep within her. It was a sensation she had never had before.

He then hugged her firmly, placing his hand on her lower back and pressing her into his body. She felt the hardness of his aroused penis pressing against her. Richard then kissed her with passion, forcing open her lips with his tongue. Never had Elizabeth been kissed like this and she returned his kiss with the same fervour.

He then slowly lowered Elizabeth onto one of the reclining deck chairs that was covered by a large soft towel. With one hand free he pushed her dress up to the waistline and placed his hand between her thighs. Elizabeth felt a wetness on her scanties as he stroked her through them. Richard's hand then thrust down into her silk underwear, and he pushed his fingers through into the soft warm opening to her vagina. She experienced an intense excruciating, throbbing sensation which she had no control over. As he massaged her clitoris, Elizabeth's body seemed to take over her mind, silently saying, "Yes, yes."

It was enough to blot out any sensible thoughts of any possible consequences of unprotected intercourse with Richard.

His voice was husky as he said, "I know you want me. Say yes. You are so beautiful and I certainly want you."

Elizabeth was still a virgin at twenty-three, and this was an urgent desire she had never experienced before. She realised Richard knew she was fully aroused. He raised himself above her briefly as he undid his trouser zip and then she was shocked at the large, red erect penis extending revealed.

Richard now was so aroused that he lost all thought for Elizabeth and he scratched her upper thigh whilst Elizabeth was struggling and fighting to lift herself up from the deck chair. Elizabeth had never seen an adult penis before let alone one so engorged. She struggled underneath his strong powerful body and managed to free her arms. As he commenced to pull down her silk scanties she slapped him hard across the face.

Her mind was now fully engaged, as she realised what was about to happen. This was not love but lust, and he was hurting her as he tried to push her back down. Had it all been planned by Richard? Why was this area so secluded and why was a towel placed on the chair?

"No, no, I canna do this! The first man that will have me will be the one I will marry," she exclaimed.

Richard was still smarting from the slap to his face as he lifted himself up from Elizabeth and angrily looked at her.

He looked so different from the man she knew the past week as he growled, "So you are just like the other tarts I've met. You lead a man on till you get a promise to marry out of him. Well I have other plans."

Elizabeth stood up and answered, "Well you'll no have me for a bit of fun. I have other plans too."

She turned and ran along the deck and down the stairwell to her cabin.

Maureen came into their cabin as Elizabeth was washing her face at the basin. She saw immediately how upset Elizabeth appeared with her reddened eyes and flushed complexion. As Elizabeth turned towards her Maureen hugged her tightly.

Elizabeth was too humiliated to tell her what had happened. She simply asked, "Can we spend some time together for the next few days, just keeping each other company?"

Two days later as they walked along the promenade, they passed Richard with his arm around a young attractive woman. He ignored Elizabeth, but she felt sorry for that young lady. Richard obviously was very experienced sexually, and she understood how easily it could happen - for young vulnerable women to be seduced by such a person.

She thought to herself, 'What a shocking thing it would be for a single woman to get pregnant on the voyage and be left at the wharf without any support!'

It so hardened Elizabeth's resolve that her experience with Richard ended any romantic adventures for her for the rest of the voyage to Melbourne. However she had to admit that the intense feeling she had experienced with Richard was one that she hoped would happen again, but only with the man she would marry one day.

For the rest of the journey Elizabeth and Maureen established a good friendship, playing deck games, walking daily along the promenade deck, and enjoying musical afternoons. They engaged in conversation with other single passengers, listening to stories of their past lives and also their hopes for a future in Australia.

Sheila and Jill spent most of their days and evenings with their male friends. They often came back to the cabin after midnight. Elizabeth and Maureen saw little of them, as often the English girls were so soundly asleep in the mornings they were hardly bothered about breakfast.

Elizabeth never mentioned why she no longer saw Richard but she did wonder if Sheila's friend Tom had spoken to her about what had happened. Sheila and Jill were close, and it was obvious that they preferred their men friends to socializing with other women.

The Londoners were friendly towards Elizabeth and Maureen and often kept them amused with the gossip they heard from the stewards about ship life among the crew and some of the passengers.

Maureen remarked to her friend, "We have nae trouble with our cabin friends, and tis a guid thing we all get along so well."

"Aye," agreed Elizabeth. "They spend so little time here, and I enjoy their gossip."

Four days after leaving Cape Town, Elizabeth suffered another bout of seasickness. The wind had whipped into a force eight gale and the pitching and rolling of the ship meant that she again was forced to stay in her cabin. Maureen again cared for her, making sure that she kept hydrated with sugared drinks.

Maureen had seen several of the passengers leaning over the deck clutching their stomachs and vomiting. She told her friend, "Well girl, you are not alone with this. There are many people suffering and they also are praying for fine weather. There were very few at breakfast this morning."

Elizabeth knew the awful symptoms would pass but that thought did not help much in her present condition. Thankfully two days later the heavy seas did abate. Elizabeth hoped that that was the last time she would ever suffer from seasickness.

She thought, 'How could I ever return to Scotland knowing that I would suffer like that again?'

For the rest of the journey across the Indian Ocean, the weather stayed fine and Elizabeth found herself enjoying the daily routine on board the *Beltana*.

It was thrilling to finally see the coastline of Australia in the distance as they prepared to dock at Fremantle. Elizabeth could not put into words her thoughts and feelings as the ship berthed. The sun beating down onto the deck felt so hot, the air was dry and very warm. As she looked across the wharf the land looked parched, but the sea was sparkling under a clear bright blue sky.

'Well,' she pondered to herself. 'This was my decision alone to leave

Scotland and there's nae turning back now. I dinna ken what I'll find in Melbourne but I know that I am strong enough to make the best of it.'

.o0o.

CHAPTER 10: Arrival

As the ship was guided to its berth at Port Melbourne, Elizabeth peered over the railing, anxiously hoping to catch a glimpse of the Cowells. So many thoughts raced through her head. 'Scotland, Scotland, what have I done? How could I leave my family? Will I ever see them again?'

Elizabeth felt as if her past was buried with absolute finality, and she would be cut off from the family forever. It filled her with excitement but also apprehension as she looked across to the wharves. Just for a brief moment Elizabeth felt as if she would do anything to persuade the Captain to allow her to head back to Scotland on the return journey.

"I've got to face it," she told herself. "I am here now, it's real and there is no going back. Only the future is important now. This is what I wanted, to get away from Dysart. For years and years mother had persuaded me to stay, but now I am twenty-three I am finally free to choose my own path."

The deep-throated sound of the tugboat brought her back to reality but tears welled up in her eyes, at the unknown future that lay ahead in this strange new land that was to be her home.

Elizabeth was standing with her suitcase waiting to disembark when she heard her name called below the gangway, and there were Doctor John and Jeannie standing in the crowd. The doctor's hair was grey and even though it was many years since Elizabeth had last seen the Cowells she had no difficulty recognizing his face.

That face was now tanned as it never had been in Scotland, and she saw age lines around his blue eyes, but his warm gentle smile and his frantic waving to get her attention gave Elizabeth enough confidence to know that she had made the right choice in arriving in Melbourne.

The breeze was warm, with a few light clouds scattered high in the sky. A light wind was gently rocking some of the fishing boats she saw across the water.

After the formalities of disembarkation the Cowells both hugged Elizabeth with joy.

Jeannie said, "We've long looked forward to this moment when we can bring you to our home and have you share your stories of your family with us."

Elizabeth had never been driven in such a comfortable car. It was the latest model Ford coupe and John Cowell had purchased it just a few months ago. It was red with black trim and leather seats. He proudly told her how he had learnt to drive on the wide roads in Melbourne and how his surgery practice was doing so well in South Yarra.

They drove down the wide tree lined boulevard of St Kilda, flanked by magnificent plane trees that were showing their rich green new growth in late spring. Elizabeth gazed at some of the large homes lining St Kilda Road. She was overwhelmed by the spaciousness of the large blocks with their beautiful gardens and very substantial homes.

John said, "Elizabeth, Melbourne is a beautiful city but, aye, there is plenty of poverty here too."

Elizabeth stared in amazement as she looked across at the magnificent gardens through the trees and she thought, 'There is no poverty to be seen though, in this part of Melbourne.'

The spacious wide road with the green painted trams running though the centre of it lifted her spirits, and she realized that Melbourne was a modern beautiful city, and to explore it one day would be a joy.

They drove into the driveway of the Cowell's home in South Yarra and Elizabeth found it hard to believe there was much poverty around this area at all. The front yard was so large that John had no difficulty passing through the wide gates and parking his car in the driveway opposite the surgery where a garage was in the process of being constructed.

Elizabeth reflected on how different this house was to the 'but and ben' her family had lived in. The front door of the old home had opened straight onto the narrow street, had only a shared toilet and laundry, and there was not a tree to be seen in the narrow cobbled streets of Dysart.

John and Jeannie had furnished Elizabeth's room with a single bed, three feet wide with a rose quilted bedspread lying on the top. A large dark stained wardrobe was in one corner of the room and a marble topped washstand was in the other corner. A wide window opened onto a side veranda and the curtains at either side of the window matched the bedspread.

Elizabeth was overwhelmed with the room. She turned to Jeannie and hugged her.

"I've never had a room of my own before, never had my own wardrobe, and what a beautiful wide bed! I canna thank you both enough, and I hope that you will find me a willing worker as well as a friend."

John smiled, turned to Elizabeth and said, "Well, tis a fine thing to have Anne's lass here at last. We have looked forward to having you share our home with us. You may also like to help me sometime in the surgery. I remember all our chats we had when you were young, and the interest you took in my medical books."

Elizabeth's eyes glowed with joy as she thought how lucky she was to finally arrive in the Cowell home and to work for them.

Two months seemed to fly as Elizabeth got used to the routine of the home. The Cowells employed a cleaner who did most of the general cleaning once per week, as well as polishing the furniture, and ironing. Elizabeth would often take a cup of tea into the surgery and if there were no patients, she would sit and quietly chat about some of the doctor's work. She learnt the routine, and often helped to organize the patients' cards and file them when John was particularly busy. Sometimes John asked her to work in the surgery, sterilizing some of his instruments, and in between patients he would discuss some of the new medical discoveries he had read about.

It was usually after 10 a.m. by the time Elizabeth finished her domestic duties: preparing breakfast, and then the monotonous daily routine of washing the dishes, cleaning and sweeping. However she was still finding her new environment stimulating, as she was spending more time during her free hours helping in the surgery. It was this time that she enjoyed so much as her mind was absorbing many new experiences.

She was also coming into contact with John's patients. They were a broad cross section of Australians who plodded in and out of the surgery each day.

These hours also dulled the ache of homesickness that had been with her since arrival. Sometimes she went to the solitude of her bedroom to self-indulgently cry the ache away. She knew there was no return to Scotland for her.

One morning Elizabeth was helping in the surgery when she spotted a man outside the door. It was obvious he was not keen to enter the waiting room. Leaning casually, with a half embarrassed expression on his face was a man in his late thirties. His hat was pulled down low over his face shielding his eyes from the gusty hot wind and the sun that was already beginning to climb high in the sky, beating down on the earth, and sucking the moisture out of the drooping plants near the surgery door. His shoes had long since lost their shine, and the weather-beaten look of them matched the collarless grubby shirt and rolled up sleeves showing probably a week of wear.

"Listen miss, you're the doctor's nurse aren't you?"

These few words in a distinctive Australian drawl reminded Elizabeth that he regarded her as someone of responsibility, and she had to make every effort to adjust and adapt to this climate, and assimilate as a new Australian. This man was what Australians referred to as an 'Aussie'. He was not the bronze, lithe, toughened Australian that the immigration posters portrayed. He was just like any working man in Scotland, except for his lack of any pretence, and the dark bronze tan of his arms. He had the same deep lines around the edges of his eyes. He wore a stained collarless striped shirt with a leather belt holding up his worn grey trousers. His air of complete casualness as he leaned against the door reminded Elizabeth of her father who'd worked so hard in the coalmines.

Before Elizabeth could reply the man said, "I rang the door bell in the front and there wasn't no answer, so you give this to the Doctor please. I saw him yesterday and he said I had to bring along a sample of my urine. Me name is Jack Reid."

A large bottle wrapped in newspaper was thrust into Elizabeth's hands and he sauntered down the drive, relieved to be rid of his embarrassing parcel. Elizabeth's mirth bubbled uncontrollably as she whisked through the waiting room, passing three patients, knocking on the doctor's door and making sure there were no patients inside. Unwrapping the bottle, Elizabeth tried to control herself and not laugh out loud. It was a beer bottle filled to the top with urine. Even the label was still on the bottle.

"I've a wee present from one of your many admirers, Dr. Cowell."

He looked up from his desk and saw the bottle in Elizabeth's outstretched hand. Through her chuckles she explained what had happened. Together they both burst into loud laughter. Even the patients in the waiting room must surely have smiled at the sounds echoing from the surgery.

"Not another of my many admirers! A wee thimble full would have been sufficient."

Her contact with many of the patients gave Elizabeth much pleasure. They were often prepared to divulge their reason for attending the surgery, treating Elizabeth with frankness and honesty.

Elizabeth felt great affection for John Cowell but it was just a close friendship between them. He had given her much of his time to help her settle into the household. However, she was beginning to pick up signals from Jeannie that were not so kind and welcoming.

As well as her time in the surgery, Elizabeth was also kept fully occupied helping Jeannie in the kitchen, baking and cooking, and doing laundry work. Occasionally she was allowed go shopping in South Yarra, which she found a delightful experience, as there was such a huge range of food available. As the Cowells had accounts at most of the stores, the cost of the items on Jeannie's list was never an issue.

There was a small strip shopping area in South Yarra of about thirty shops and Elizabeth loved to wander along it. The cake shop was where the bread was purchased and it had a wide choice of pies, cakes and pastries. Elizabeth loved the smell of the freshly cooked meat pies and sausage rolls, the mouth-watering cake display of treats such as lamingtons, custard tarts and sponges. She had never seen such displays in Dysart, nor had sampled meat pies like the ones baked here.

Gradually Elizabeth learnt the names of the owners who usually served in the shops. Mr Forsyth's chemist shop had a large apothecary bottle in the front window. He would say to her, "I've made up some garlic medicine for Mrs Cowell, and a tonic that Doctor Cowell has ordered."

As he wrapped up the medicines he would remark to other customers, "We've a fine doctor now in South Yarra and this lass often helps in his surgery. If you or your family have asthma or any other illness I can recommend Doctor Cowell."

Elizabeth felt proud to be regarded as part of the family and to hear the glowing praise for Doctor Cowell.

Next door to the chemist there was a 'ham and beef' shop. Sometimes Elizabeth would ask for a "hot roast rabbit and a pound of best butter, please."

Mr Corr would hand over the rabbit with a carton of hot gravy, then the butter and say, "Mrs Cowell must be making shortbread. She's a fine Scottish lady."

Sometimes Elizabeth would bring in a couple of pieces for Mr Corr to enjoy.

Jeannie did enjoy making buttery, delicious shortbread, as it was such a favourite of her husband for his morning tea.

Sometimes the butcher would say, "Tell her I got a nice hock and my lad will bring it with the weekend meat - I know how much they enjoy pea and ham soup."

The fish shop was next. The window had water running down the glass and held piled up crayfish, bottles of pickled onions and mussels ready for Friday night shopping. Elizabeth was amazed that here everybody could afford crayfish, as it was plentiful in the ocean only fifty miles from South Yarra. Workers would share transport to head there at weekends and throw in craypots. The crayfish in the window were huge and the Cowells and Elizabeth usually had one on Fridays. What a treat it was for Elizabeth, especially as she had never had such a succulent treat in Scotland.

The lending library was also in the shopping strip and for a penny or two Elizabeth often borrowed books there, chosen by the owner. Elizabeth loved reading, and Mrs Lamb often purchased titles that Elizabeth would ask for. She especially enjoyed some of the Australian authors such as Ethel Turner and Mary Grant Bruce, as well as the *Jaina* series by the Canadian Mazo de la Roche.

Elizabeth would enter the grocer's shop and hand over the order that was to be delivered, and as it was such a generous order Mr Blackman would hand Elizabeth a small bag of broken biscuits. The shop keepers liked listening to Elizabeth's broad Scottish accent, and found this new lass to South Yarra very attractive with her wide generous smile and rich black curly hair. They enjoyed talking briefly to her and they in turn opened her eyes to life in Melbourne as they told her of some of their tough times settling in and becoming accepted.

The greengrocer had buckets of poppies and gum tips outside the door. Con the greengrocer could not read English and Elizabeth would read out the order. He would put the vegetables into the basket and say to Elizabeth, "Tella Mrs Cowell I bringa da blackcurrants, two boxes, for you. Mrs Cowell want nice navels - they here for her."

The homesickness still persisted though. That Christmas, in the afternoon the turkey lay cold and untouched with the roast vegetables filling the large tureen. Elizabeth could smell the sweet aroma of the rich Christmas pudding that had been made a few days before. Never had she seen so much dried fruit and fine ingredients mixed into it, including cherries and brandy, eight eggs, and a generous amount of butter. What would her mother think of such extravagance? Elizabeth remembered the fresh cod that they ate so often and the suet pudding made in Scotland with just a few currents and shared with much delight among her family. She bent her head and sobbed.

The Cowells were out visiting friends. In their absence the silence of the house overwhelmed Elizabeth as she thought of her mother, her brother Robert and her two sisters sharing Christmas together.

"Och, what I would give to be with them now."

This first Australian Christmas ought to be a wonderful, memorable one and yet it was the most miserable one Elizabeth could ever remember. The desire to return home completely engulfed her, blocking out all reasoning. 'If this is homesickness, this feeling of complete misery and sadness, then please let it pass, for while I feel like this nothing is worth doing or struggling for. It cannae be a land of promise, a land of the future when I feel like this,' she thought.

It made Elizabeth feel like telling the pompous immigrant officials who had interviewed her, what to do with their words. They had fooled her and she hoped that not many more migrants would be fooled into taking such a gamble coming to Australia.

Slowly she put the food into the large refrigerator that had been recently purchased. It was one of the newest electric models with an ice cube compartment. It was an expensive purchase and Elizabeth knew that it would be many years before most families could afford one.

Before the new purchase, and for many other folks still, the iceman would come each day to replace the block of ice in the icebox. In hot weather especially it was not a very efficient way to keep food from spoiling. Now

Elizabeth did not need to shop at the butcher's quite so often and the new refrigerator kept the milk, butter, cream and cheese cold and very fresh. Cold comfort for a homesick heart.

.o0o.

CHAPTER 11: A Moment Of Clarity

The Richards family had invited the Cowells out to Christmas lunch the previous day. Doctor Richards lived in Toorak and over the past five years had become a valuable friend to John Cowell. They frequently shared medical information and discussed treatments they had given some of their patients. Dr. Richards had also established a successful practice and the two families met fortnightly, usually at one of the local restaurants.

Jeannie was now in her early fifties and her blond hair, now streaked with grey, was kept tied into a bun. Age lines had developed around her eyes and her slackening neck muscles were also showing the signs of ageing. Menopause had not been kind to Jeannie. She had put on several pounds over the past seven years and it showed with her thickening waist and slightly bulging stomach.

Jeannie had observed Elizabeth and John's close friendly relationship developing over the past four months. She was envious of the youthfulness of Elizabeth, and her fresh pale skin, coal black curly hair and slim figure. Jeannie had lately treated Elizabeth with coldness and started giving her tasks such as cleaning the bathroom and polishing the floors – tasks that had previously been done by the cleaner.

She resented John often calling Elizabeth into the surgery to help as his nurse when he was busy. Jeannie was determined that Elizabeth would not accompany them to share the Christmas lunch with their friends, and made it clear to John that she was not to be invited. John felt guilty leaving Elizabeth on her own but he had assured her they would share Christmas tea with her.

Elizabeth flung herself down onto the soft eiderdown on her bed. What was it she longed for? There was an ache that seemed to be causing her such grief. No, it wasn't a matter of missing the Scotland she remembered. She couldn't miss the depressing greyness of the tenements rising up from the narrow cobbled road, the door of each of those tenements leading into the tiny overcrowded rooms, nor miss the filthy slimy toilets and the cramped laundries shared by the families who lived in those 'but and bens'.

It wasn't Dysart with its dank air and the long dark winters, with coal dust hanging in the air and at times making even breathing difficult. Not the heaps of coal slag, and the mines that dominated the small towns and the lives of the people along the Firth. The poverty of the workers and the terrible accidents that happened so often destroying so many families - these were bleak memories Elizabeth would never forget.

Had not a yearning to free herself from all that life been with her for many years? It was almost as if Elizabeth could reach out and touch yesterday – touch the memories of her home, and that small room above Mrs McKenna's dress shop. The place where for seven years she had bowed her head over a sewing machine struggling with poor light, or hand-sewed costumes, clothes and thousands of sequins and beads onto the bodices of dresses for the wealthy women of the district, mainly mine owners' wives.

A clarity of thought suddenly filled Elizabeth's head. It was her mother. That was who she missed. Somehow she just had to convince her mother to make the long journey to Melbourne. And that would surely then encourage her brother Robert to follow with her two sisters. Mother was the pivot. If Elizabeth could persuade her mother Anne to make the journey then all her family would surely follow.

With that thought fixed firmly in her mind from that point, Elizabeth's bank balance gradually grew till she had fifty pounds deposited.

It was now six months since she had started work at the Cowells'. When Elizabeth helped in the surgery, John Cowell would give her an extra pound as often she helped him late in the evening with the cleaning of the surgery, being very particular to make sure that it was spotless for the patients the next day.

John Cowell enjoyed having Elizabeth work with him, but Jeannie had gradually come to resent it. She had heard him remark, "Och lassie, if ye had been my daughter then you would be a doctor ye self now. There's no doubt ye are smart, young lassie. We did miss you when you shifted awa tae Dysart."

Elizabeth had written several letters to her mother trying to persuade her to move, cajoling and pleading with her to break her ties with Scotland and all of the sad memories that the 'Old Country' held for her.

Jeannie also wrote to Anne, describing her own life and the opportunities that Robert, Janet and Fay would have in Melbourne. For all her growing resentment of Elizabeth – a resentment that she knew in her heart was unfounded and unfair – she still held a great fondness for her old school friend, and missed her companionship.

At last Anne consented to come to Melbourne. Elizabeth knew that once she had started the formalities for immigration, with the help of John Cowell, her sisters and brother would follow. Her mother was a dominating person, but she loved them and had tried hard to give them a better life than the one she had had as a miner's wife. Anne knew that Robert certainly did not have much of a future in the mines. Gradually the mines in the district were closing. The coal ships were no longer coming into the small harbour in Dysart and many miners were losing their jobs. Anne was also terrified of losing Robert to a mine accident just as she had lost his father. Perhaps that was the reason that finally persuaded the matriarch to migrate to Melbourne.

Melbourne now seemed to take on new meaning. Elizabeth looked outside her window and took in the clear blue sky, the scent of the gum trees, the sound of the birds. She thought of the shops with their abundance of such a wide variety of food that was affordable to workers on basic wages - wages that were protected by laws.

Elizabeth vowed to herself, "I will work to bring out my family. I shall put up with the unfriendliness of Mrs Cowell, as it is only through this family I will eventually save enough to help assist my family out. I will need to rent a home and furnish it for them as well."

Elizabeth had often looked in the paper and found that rents in Richmond and Burnley were cheap as they were mainly workers' homes surrounded by many factories - shoes, clothing, processed food and heavy engineering. Those suburbs seemed to be where the future lay.

.o0o.

CHAPTER 12: Exploring Melbourne

Her Sundays were free for Elizabeth to explore around South Yarra and she headed out along Bridge Road on the tram to Richmond. As she wandered down Burnley Street from Bridge Road and down close to the Yarra River she saw there was a huge change in the housing for working families. What a contrast to where the Cowells lived, and it opened her eyes to the poverty in inner Melbourne.

As Elizabeth walked down towards the river she could hear the mournful bellowing of the cattle behind the corrugated iron wall of the abattoir, and the stench of the animals was overwhelming. She was shocked to see cattle being led down the road from the Burnley Station.

As she wandered into one of the laneways there were three children playing there on the bluestone cobbles. Their hair was unkempt, and their clothing very dirty. They opened their back gate and ran inside when they saw her. Through the open gate she observed a very small yard where their mother was washing in a trough at the back of the house. The woman then emptied the trough onto the dirt, leaving the scum to puddle around her feet. There was no drainage leading away from the back of the house.

"Och, even our wee home in Dysart was a palace compared to these homes," Elizabeth quietly said to herself.

The area was unsewered, and the flap at the back of the pan toilet wall was hanging from a rusted hinge. These flaps of the toilets opening onto the lanes obviously provided access for the 'pan man' who carried the stinking pans and loaded them onto his cart. Three of the homes were built of corrugated iron. They were small and probably only consisted of three rooms, and she imagined how hot it must be inside in the Melbourne summer and how cold in winter.

The abattoir near the river provided work for hundreds of men but Elizabeth could not imagine the working conditions of the men as they slaughtered the animals. The bellowing of the cattle locked into their fate saddened and distressed Elizabeth and she walked quickly back to Bridge Road.

'Just as well I wandered down here as I would never rent a home for mother in this area,' she thought. Closer to the shopping area on Bridge Road in Richmond, the quality of the houses improved considerably and Elizabeth wrote down the names of some of the streets to remind herself of rental possibilities. Richmond was close to South Yarra but she knew that her family would not be able to afford to rent near the Cowells' home, which was close to Como House, a huge mansion owned by the Armytage family.

John Cowell had spoken to her of the magnificent gardens, and the huge mansion. John and Jeannie had been invited there once to a lavish garden party given by the Armytages to raise funds for the Queen Victoria Hospital in Melbourne which was established to be 'operated by women for women.' Little could Elizabeth know what an important part that hospital would play in her life when she was in her thirties.

Elizabeth saw some 'for rent' homes advertised in the window of one of the shops. In upper Richmond they were much bigger than her home in Dysart, and each home had its own inside bathroom, toilet and laundry with a concrete washbasin and a copper. Most of the homes in Richmond were built of weatherboard with cantilevered verandas at their front, or were brick homes joined by a shared wall, with a long passage on either side of the shared wall. They had three rooms apart from a kitchen and inside bathroom. In parts of Richmond the houses even had sewered toilets.

'Yes,' she thought, 'I am sure that I will find a suitable home near here for Mother. She could walk to the shops here, or catch a tram into Melbourne one day.' The trams in Melbourne were called W class trams and Elizabeth enjoyed travelling on them, as they were new with comfortable padded seats and wooden fittings. The tramlines were rapidly being extended as far out as Wattle Park, which she hoped to visit soon.

Elizabeth was determined not to let Jeannie Cowell and her pettiness towards her get her down as it was vital that she remain at the Cowells'. She knew that she was safe there as John Cowell loved having Elizabeth in their home, sharing conversations of life in Dunfermline, and she made sure that she followed Jeannie's instructions diligently. The small wage of two pounds gave her enough to save a pound a week.

Jeannie provided Elizabeth's black dress and white aprons, but made it known at every opportunity to her visitors that Elizabeth was her domestic servant. As Elizabeth had always been independent since starting her dressmaking apprenticeship so many years ago, it made her squirm inside to have to accept the sarcastic cutting remarks, which were always said out of John Cowell's hearing.

"Och look at that dust in the corner of the lounge. I told you to mop it this morning. The wash basin in the bathroom was not clean enough," Jeannie would criticize.

Elizabeth realized that Mrs Cowell was probably suffering from problems with menopause as her face was often flushed with perspiration and dampness around her hairline. She had looked up the symptoms in one of John's medical books, and instead of resenting Jeannie's cruel comments, Elizabeth perhaps felt some pity towards her.

John was so absorbed with his practice, his patients, and the study he needed to do to keep up with the new developments in medicine, that he did not notice his wife's changed attitude towards Elizabeth. Jeannie deeply envied the youthfulness of Elizabeth, her beautiful cream unblemished complexion and the long black hair without a trace of grey. She knew that her fear of losing John was irrational. He had never shown the slightest romantic interest in Elizabeth. The young woman was always treated by John with kindness and as the daughter they had never had. He would never allow Jeannie to force Elizabeth to leave their home.

Mrs Cowell was nonetheless frightened of losing her husband's affection, which he had always given with a gentle tolerance. It was his desire to leave Dunfermline when Jeannie had been so reluctant that gave him such patience with her when she was angry or upset over some minor incident. He knew how much Jeannie missed her family, friends and the familiarity of the city she loved. Many times Jeannie spoke to him of her longing to visit Scotland again.

John knew that he would never go back as he loved his new environment. He loved his adopted land, and his practice was very successful. He knew, too, that Jeannie would find Scotland very different if she ever returned, as people simply moved on with their lives. Some of their friends had since died. They would certainly be welcomed by some who remembered them, but he believed that it was far more likely that they would more often now be treated with the friendliness accorded to passing visitors. Much time had passed, and he knew that people in Dunfermline would have moved on with their lives, just as he had moved on with his own.

.o0o.

CHAPTER 13: Sewing Again

Elizabeth drowsily opened her eyes to a new day. For the first time in weeks she felt a new optimism about her future and a lightness in her heart. Now she had a real purpose to strive for.

The huge branches of the gum tree stretched its shade to shield her window from the strong Australian sunlight, and swayed gently in the warm northerly wind. Elizabeth loved that huge gum, the scent of the eucalyptus, the wide girth of the trunk and the bird life that was attracted to the blossoms. She was entranced by the brilliant colour of the plumage of the parrots.

These hot north winds were still unfamiliar to Elizabeth but she knew that by late morning all of the curtains would be drawn across and the blinds pulled down to help keep the house cool throughout the day. Luckily the house had wide verandas which made a great difference to the inside temperature.

However on these days Jeannie became angry as she perspired and found that it was impossible to venture out to the shops, or even outside. With the extra weight she now carried, on hot days Jeannie could not bear to wear the corset that helped her regain some of her lost figure.

It had been a month ago when Jeannie had travelled to Myer in Melbourne and purchased the latest elasticized *Berlei* pale pink corset. It was worn pulled up just below her bust, with extra elastic material supporting the stomach area, and the length of the corset extending just above the thighs. The suspenders were joined to her corset and Jeannie had attached them to her silk stockings. They were all terribly uncomfortable with the long bloomers she wore and she wished she had purchased the short modern 'scanties' she saw in Myers.

Elizabeth noticed that now Jeannie had removed her stockings and corset and had put on a shorter, dropped waist dress that was currently fashionable. Jeannie had her hair cut short into a 'bob' graduating from the back of her neck to her chin with a soft fringe across her forehead and soft curls around her ears.

Elizabeth was impressed by the new hairstyle. She said, "It is going to be a hot one today, but I do like your new hair style. And that lovely dress will help keep you cool, as it is so light and bright."

Jeannie smiled at Elizabeth's compliment and said, "There's a wonderful hair stylist in South Yarra who is up to date with the new hair styles. I was worried about how it would suit me, but it is much easier to manage now that my lengthy locks have been cut off."

"Well it suits you, and I am sure Doctor John will like your new look as well."

Jeannie's new dress gave Elizabeth an idea - to use her sewing skills and advertise herself as a dressmaker. She desperately needed to earn extra money to help with the family's assisted passage and furnish a home for them when they arrived.

The dropped waist style would be easy to copy and some of the women around South Yarra were already wearing those fashionable dresses. With the new crepe de chine, taffeta, velvet and silk fabrics now becoming cheaper and widely available, she could make them at an affordable cost to appeal to a wide cross section of women.

Before she left Scotland Elizabeth had made herself a winter coat with a shawl collar lapel and the belt attached below the waistline, in a soft grey woollen material. When she had worn it along Toorak Road to the local shops it was much admired by some of the customers.

Mrs McKenna, Elizabeth's Scottish employer in the early 1920s, had seen magazine pictures of the French couturier Mademoiselle Chanel and she had persuaded some of her clients to have dresses made in the simple style using crepe de chine as the fabric. It was soft and draped smoothly over the hips.

Elizabeth had sewed a dress in the dropped waist style with fitted sleeves and had added some gilt buttons for effect for one of the clients. She knew that the line of the dress was very important. It had to be plain, but perfect with just a little decoration, as she had seen on some of the Chanel designs in the fashion magazines and in the *Butterick* patterns they were using in Mrs McKenna's shop. Elizabeth started to cut out some of the new designs in the *Vogue, Everyladies* and *Australian Home Journal* magazines she purchased. She had also brought out some of the *Butterick* patterns that she had used in Scotland.

It was by chance when she walked into the chemist shop to collect Jeannie's prescription she overheard one of the customers remarking to Mrs Forsyth, "Yes, I do love the new fashions and the shorter dresses with the softer fabrics, but with my figure I will need to find a dressmaker to make one to fit me."

Elizabeth could hardly believe this opportunity. It might give her the chance to show her skills to the local women!

"Excuse me," she said. "I heard your discussion and I would love to design and sew a modern dress for you. I served my apprenticeship for four years in Scotland and sewed for many of my employer's clients. I can measure, cut a pattern to fit you, and make the dress. The new fabrics are wonderful to wear."

"Oh, you are the lass my husband talks about," the woman replied. "I know that you work for the Cowell family, and they live near us. I would be thrilled if you could manage to sew a dress for me."

Elizabeth's eyes lit up at the thought of restarting her dressmaking. But she suddenly realised that there was a problem.

'What was I thinking of?' she said to herself. 'I dinna have a sewing machine!'

She turned to Mr Forsyth who had listened to their conversation and said, "Would ye mind if I put a wee advert in your shop window, looking for a Singer treadle sewing machine?"

Mrs Forsyth turned to Elizabeth and smiled as she said, "My mother has a sewing machine and it is quite a while since she last used it. I am sure she will want to get it out of her home. She would be pleased to meet you. Perhaps you could sew a dress for my mother, as it is difficult for her to purchase her dresses to fit her fuller figure. Mother lives two streets away from the Cowell home and I would be happy to take you there. My husband often talks about the friendly Scottish lass that visits his shop and

I am sure my mother also would enjoy meeting you."

Three days later Elizabeth was the proud owner of a Singer treadle dressmakers' model sewing machine in an oak cabinet, with two drawers on either side of the treadle and a fold out oak lid. It was decided that Elizabeth would pay twenty pounds for the machine over a period of one year. It looked new, as although Mrs Forsyth's mother had not used it for several years she had kept it in excellent condition.

It was very similar to the one Elizabeth had used in Scotland and she had found it ideal for sewing tricky materials such as velvet or heavy woollen fabrics, as when she pushed the pedal the machine just made one stitch, and she was able to guide the fabric slowly around tricky corners of the garment.

The chemist's mother-in-law, Mrs Crosby, proved to be very happy with the transaction, and took an interest in Elizabeth's proposed new venture.

"Now dear, where are you going to set up your dressmaking?" the older woman asked, and then suddenly continued, "I have an idea. I live alone, and I have two spare rooms at the back of my home. For a small rent you can set up your business there. If you can manage to do some sewing for me, then you can rent the rooms for one pound a week."

Once that was agreed to, the new benefactor said, "Well now that we have you set up, would you like to accompany me to the Myer Emporium in Melbourne next week? We can choose some fabric and a pattern. It is a huge establishment and it has a vast range of fabrics. We could investigate some of the new couture dresses for some ideas, as Myer caters also for very wealthy people, as well as ordinary customers who enjoy browsing and shopping in the Emporium."

During supper that evening Elizabeth shyly told of her plans to set up her dressmaking business. She spoke carefully, making sure that Jeannie would also benefit.

"I will sew in the evenings and on my free day at the weekend. I would like to have the opportunity to make a costume or dress for you, Jeannie. It would be at a much cheaper cost than the dress you recently purchased. I wish to bring my family out from Scotland and I need to earn the money by dressmaking for some of the local women in South Yarra."

Jeannie looked across at John and saw his eyes light up at Elizabeth's new venture.

"Aye it is a grand idea, and I have heard of your talents from your mother in her letters to Jeannie," said the doctor warmly.

Jeannie thought about her friend Anne who now may get the opportunity to come to Melbourne. It would also keep Elizabeth so busy that she would have little time to help John in his surgery.

"What a grand idea Elizabeth," she agreed. "I am sure that once some of the local women have seen their friends wearing your designs, you will be a great success."

The following Saturday Elizabeth and old Mrs Crosby met at the tram stop near Punt Road and a few minutes later boarded one of the new W class trams. The tram travelled along the wide St. Kilda Boulevard. The route looked magnificent with the tall plane trees on either side shading the road with their bright green leaves, out in full colour in the late summer. Most of the homes bordering the road were impressive huge stone Edwardian mansions two storeys high, surrounded by beautiful treed gardens.

This was the first time Elizabeth had visited the City. They passed Flinders Street Station with the clocks highlighting the magnificent Edwardian entrance, and the outside of the enormous building painted in a dark yellow. Hundreds of people were disgorging out of the station and her eyes could hardly take in the busy scene. The huge station building extended down Flinders Street, and diagonally opposite, she saw the bluestone St Pauls Cathedral. It was as grand as the cathedral in Dunfermline but Elizabeth commented that it lacked spires.

Mrs Crosby looked across and said, "It is the Anglican Cathedral. Work is commencing on the construction of three spires, which will certainly make it the most magnificent Cathedral in Australia."

Elizabeth turned to Mrs Crosby and replied happily, "Melbourne is an impressive city - I canna wait to explore more of it myself."

They alighted at Bourke Street and walked down to the Myer Emporium with its long street frontage.

Mrs Crosby said, "I now shop at Myer about once a fortnight. They have expanded the store recently, and have opened a new section in Lonsdale Street, which will be twelve floors. It is a marvellous place to shop as they import goods and fashion clothing from all over Europe. Myer now owns woollen mills and clothing factories in Victoria.

"My friend's husband is a manager in the men's wear section and he receives paid vacations. There has even been a sick fund instituted, and there is a free hospital within the store. The staff members enjoy many social activities provided by Myer as well. My friend and her husband went to a staff ball recently and a picnic at the beach last week funded by the Company. He does enjoy working for this Company as they do look after their staff - nearly 2000 employees."

The footpath was crowded with people and it was obvious that this street was the heart of Melbourne for shoppers and day trippers. They passed several other large stores as they walked, such as 'Buckley and Nunn' and 'Foy and Gibson's'.

The Myer Emporium, with its impressive window displays, vast interiors and open counters displaying such a range of goods could not help but entice people to spend. The signage at the escalators indicated that there were well over one hundred departments within the store. It was almost too overwhelming for Elizabeth to comprehend such a modern store of this size anywhere in the world.

Elizabeth knew she would be shopping in Bourke Street frequently in the future for most of her tailoring supplies. She looked forward to exploring some of the other stores as they also had large frontages with enticing window displays.

The two women made their way towards the lifts. Elizabeth had never entered a lift. As the lift doors opened a man dressed in a smart uniform greeted them. He was seated on a stool. He directed them to the third floor: "Ladies fashions, ladies undergarments, drapery, sewing patterns."

There was a vast array of dress material set out: silks, crepes, cottons, lace, taffeta, fabrics, and rayon. What was surprising was how cheap it was. Silk was about ten shillings a yard, rayon three shillings and cotton about three shillings. Elizabeth was amazed at the quality and range of fabrics, and she knew that she could make a silk dress including the fabric for about ten pounds.

They wandered over to the pattern section and browsed through the *Vogue* and *Butterick* styles. Mrs Crosby chose patterns for a suit and a dress in the modern twenties style. The styles on offer were mainly low waisted with fullness at the hemline, or they were 'shift' type dress designs.

They then selected a mauve crepe for the suit and pale green silk for the dress. Next they purchased silk and cotton thread to match the chosen fabric, and lace trimmings.

The two women made their way to the ladies' couture dress section on one of the upper floors. Elizabeth was shocked at the price tags on some of the dresses - ranging from thirty to eighty pounds.

'No wonder I can make a profit with my sewing,' she mused later. 'There must be hundreds of very wealthy women in Melbourne who can afford these prices, as there was a large range of designer dresses.'

The textures and colours of the dress designs were exciting, and they were beautifully cut in the wonderful new fabrics she had seen. Elizabeth observed that many of the dresses were also shorter, coming to just the bottom of the knees. The women wandering through this department were very stylishly dressed, wearing the latest styles, and there were several staff attending to the clients.

Elizabeth was amazed at the beautiful evening clothes displayed on the models. They were in luxurious fabrics; mostly silks, velvets, taffetas, satins and flowing chiffons. The dresses were designed to move, obviously while dancing. Some had long trailing sashes, or asymmetric hemlines. The accessories for the head were scarves in silk or bandeaux or fancy combs.

The lightness of the fabrics and the use of colour thrilled Elizabeth. She knew she had the skills to create these modern designs. Her apprenticeship in tailoring, cutting and dressmaking gave her much confidence in her ability to sew for the middle class women of South Yarra and Toorak.

Mrs Crosby took Elizabeth to the millinery department where she purchased a cloche hat and silk stockings to match the dress fabrics she had purchased.

"Now, let me take you for lunch in the Myer Cafeteria," the older woman offered.

They took the lift, and although Elizabeth noted how crowded the cafeteria was, they found a table for two. The waitressing staff were efficient and polite and the lunch excellent. It was no wonder that a visit to the Myer Emporium was a special day out for Melbournians.

John Cowell had now employed a handy man who also maintained the garden. The doctor decided to close the surgery on the weekends as he wished to discover some of the outer areas of Melbourne with Jeannie in their new car. Places like Healesville, Mornington, and Sorrento were popular and he hoped that such outings would help Jeannie to overcome her mild depression.

Jeannie had mellowed towards Elizabeth as her dressmaking was now occupying so much of her free time in the evenings and at weekends. John had also recently employed a receptionist so Elizabeth's presence was not needed in the surgery.

Jeannie was also keen to make use of Elizabeth's dressmaking skills, as she had put on several pounds around her hips and stomach and she needed well cut clothing. The dropped waist style would hide her larger hips and she looked forward to visits to Myer to select styles and fabrics with some advice from Elizabeth.

Elizabeth had finished the crepe dress for Mrs Crosby within a week. She put lace trim around the neckline and attached the loose fitting sleeves perfectly onto the bodice of the dress. On the lower section of the dropped waist dress, Elizabeth cut the material on a bias, so that it was more fluid, and draped perfectly just below the knee level. The bias cut also meant that the fabric did not fray, and helped to give a slimmer silhouette to the dress. She used matching lace trim on the cuffs, which had two small covered buttons with tiny buttonholes.

Mrs Crosby had three fittings before the dress was completed, and she was thrilled with it.

"I could never purchase one that looked so modern and fitted my figure so well, Elizabeth. Yes, you are a wonderful dressmaker and I will proudly tell my friends about your skills."

Mrs Crosby thought twelve pounds was very reasonable for a dress of that quality, as she knew it would have been over thirty pounds in the Myer store. Elizabeth had made five pounds and it was nearly twice her weekly pay working for the Cowells.

"If I can sew at least one dress each week then with what I already have, I'll have five hundred pounds saved in a year. That will be more than enough to help assist my mother and sisters out from Scotland, and furnish a rented cottage for them."

Elizabeth knew that she had the skill and the will to sew, and was excited at the possibility of having her family with her in just over a year.

It was that dress that set Elizabeth on her path as a much sought-after dressmaker. Mrs Crosby wore it to Christ Church in South Yarra on the following Sunday. The Church was a landmark with its bell tower and high spire. Inside was a chancel for the choir, and an apse for the high altar. The members of the congregation were mainly upper middle class, or wealthy patrons and were proud of their classical style building.

Mrs Crosby and her daughter and son-in-law the Forsyths persuaded Elizabeth to attend on Sunday mornings. It was an impressive church, and Elizabeth started attending regularly. It was also where she met many of her clients, and their daughters.

The Forsyths gave dinner parties regularly and some of their friends were very wealthy. The wives often wore couture dresses, but as some of them had larger figures they also became clients of Elizabeth.

Mrs Crosby was proud of her new dressmaker and promoted Elizabeth to her friends who also had daughters keen to wear the latest twenties designs. They required many dresses of different fabrics and colours to remain fashionable among their friends. In the twenties young middle class women expected to change their outfits frequently, and have new dresses for new seasons in the most current fashions. Because dress fabrics were so cheap compared to purchased clothing, Elizabeth started dressmaking for many of the young women who enjoyed choosing the bright colourful fabrics and patterns themselves. She usually made a profit of five pounds on every dress she sewed.

Within six months her bank balance had grown to three hundred pounds and she knew that she could finally afford to search for a cottage to rent by the end of year.

.o0o.

CHAPTER 14: The Macraes Come To Melbourne

Anne, Robert, Fay and Janet received Elizabeth's letter in November 1928 persuading them to start preparing to leave Scotland for Australia.

The lease on the miner's 'but and ben' was about to expire as it was now four years since Alexander had been killed. Robert had learnt that the Lady Blanche mine pit was closing, and as they were now able to apply for assisted passages sponsored by the Cowells with financial help from Elizabeth, the decision to migrate was an easy one to make.

The Cowells and Elizabeth were informed by the migration authorities that her mother would not receive an assisted passage and the fare would be ninety-five pounds, but her sisters would be assisted, as the Cowells had arranged for them to work as domestics. Robert was also to receive assisted passage as he was to work at the local brewery in Richmond, a job that had been organized by John Cowell.

It took six months before all the paper work was done, and the family was to leave Scotland in June 1929. Anne found it difficult to leave Dysart where she had found so much support from the families after Alexander had died.

"Och I dinna ken what we will find in Melbourne, but we canna stay here any longer without a home to rent," she admitted. "I long to see Elizabeth again, and Jeannie's letters have meant much to me. Now our friendship will be renewed."

Robert was thrilled to have the chance of a new start and Elizabeth had assured them that she would have a home waiting for them upon their arrival. Janet and Fay were working long hours weaving at the linen factory and they both agreed that new opportunities would await them in Melbourne, especially with Elizabeth's help.

Elizabeth started searching around the suburbs of inner Melbourne. South Yarra, Richmond and Burnley had workers' cottages near the train and tram lines. There were many factories in the area; tanneries, a large brewery, boot, soap, matches, food processing, jam and sauce factories and also foundries with engineering works nearby. From the outset of her search, Elizabeth thought to herself that her brother and sisters would have little trouble finding work here, should they be unhappy with what their sponsors had arranged..

She caught the tram along Bridge Road into the heart of Richmond, and as she looked out of the window she saw that it was a substantial shopping area. The Town Hall was an impressive elaborate building with a clock tower over one hundred feet high. There were several churches and many hotels.

It brought back memories of Dysart, and the drinking after the mine shifts that caused so much poverty in the families where so little money was saved for food. 'Well, where there are lots of hotels, there must be plenty of work as that is where they will go after their shift,' Elizabeth reasoned.

On one of her previous searches Elizabeth had walked into the large store called 'Dimmeys' in Swan Street, Richmond. She had purchased fabrics there. It had a high fashion status in Richmond. Some of her clients shopped there frequently, as it was very convenient to South Yarra. The first floor had workshops and mail order services for country people. The store was easily seen from a distance with its high, distinctive clock tower topped by a huge globe with red glass panels. Elizabeth had seen it at night glowing red in the distance from the park near the Cowell's home.

The houses near Bridge Road were built of brick and were much more liveable than where Elizabeth had wandered previously to the south of Burnley Street near the river. She had been shocked at the poverty and the condition of some of the homes, which were mainly wooden, low lying, with smelly pan toilets backing onto laneways and all lacking drainage. She remembered from her last visit the stench and noise of the abattoirs permeating the air.

Near the top of Burnley Street Elizabeth saw that the double villas were constructed of brick with verandas and a small garden in the front. They were neat and very close to transport with the Burnley rail station not too far away. The tram lines in Bridge Road and Swan Street were also close. 'My mother would like it here as she is used to living close to other families, and she would enjoy shopping in Bridge Road.'

One of the villas had a 'for rent' notice on its wooden fence and Elizabeth wrote down the phone number.

The following weekend she inspected it with the agent and was thrilled to see it had three bedrooms and a lounge room off the long passageway, with a shared wall to the villa next door. The passage led to a kitchen with an enclosed laundry at the rear of the house, with two concrete troughs and a copper at the side. Elizabeth was thrilled to find that the house was sewered, and that the rent was a very manageable two pounds a week.

She signed the rental agreement for one year in January 1929, deciding that she would move out of the Cowells' house as soon as she could furnish this home. She scoured the second hand shops mainly along Bridge Road and found that fifty pounds was sufficient to buy three single beds and a double, a tapestry lounge, a kitchen suite of wooden table and chairs, and an ice chest.

The Cowells were sorry that Elizabeth was leaving their home but they promised to employ her as their domestic for three days a week as she had been so valuable to them and was an excellent Scottish cook.

John Cowell had decided to set up a combined practice in South Yarra with his friend Doctor Ian Richards, as they both realized that the arrangement would allow them more time away. Together they could afford to hire a nurse as well as a full time receptionist, and give each other support when needed. Jeannie found John more relaxed now that he was working with Ian Richards. She enjoyed the weekend trips that they shared and Melbourne was now the place that was her home. Jeannie realized her behaviour towards Elizabeth at times had been selfish and mean.

'I don't know why I ever though of Elizabeth a threat to me,' she thought. 'I now realize that my jealousy was just irrational and I will try to help the family adjust to their new life here.' She remembered how hard she had found it in 1918 when she and John had first arrived.

Jeannie Cowell was excited at the thought of her friend Anne finally arriving in Melbourne, and provided Elizabeth with sufficient sheets, towels and linen for her house. She also cleaned out the unwanted equipment in her kitchen and provided Elizabeth with most of the cooking appliances. Jeannie had replaced much of her cooking equipment with modern stainless steel since settling into their home at South Yarra.

It was a spring afternoon in mid September 1929 when Elizabeth stood on the wharf at Port Melbourne and watched the ship *Jervis Bay* being towed towards the dockside. She could hardly contain her excitement and her heart seemed to beat at twice the normal pace. It was now over two years since she had left Scotland. The prospect of being held and hugged tightly by her mother - with all the joy and tenderness that only her mother could give, gave her such happiness. Elizabeth was also full of deep satisfaction at what she had achieved in those years.

A home was now ready for the family, furnished fully with all essential requirements for comfortable living. Elizabeth knew her mother would be thrilled when she saw it. It far exceeded in comfort the one she had lived in in Dysart.

She wished the *Jervis Bay* had a dozen tugs to manoeuvre the ship into its dock. She was sure her heart would burst waiting for the vessel's final push into the berthing spot. 'Those two small tugs appear to be taking forever,' she thought.

It took half an hour of trying to remain patient before she saw her mother, brother, and her sisters waving from the deck, and then another half hour before they descended down the gangway. There were hundred of groups greeting each other at the dockside but Elizabeth paid attention to no one else as she forced her way through the crowd.

As she walked towards her mother she saw that she hadn't changed much at all from the woman she had held so dearly in her memory for two years.

Her mother was wearing the black dress that Elizabeth had made for her four years ago. It was fitted around the bust line with small gathers across the shoulders. Elizabeth had chosen small decorative black buttons for the top section. The skirt went well below her knees and the fitted sleeves were puffed at the shoulders. It had been Anne's best dress. Elizabeth remembered how pleased her mother had been with it and only wore it on Sunday to church. It still looked smart and it suited Anne's figure well.

Elizabeth thought that it would not be too long before she would be sewing dresses more suited to Melbourne's weather for her mother. Perhaps she had gained some more weight on the voyage and her long hair was now completely grey and held into a tidy bun at the back of her head. Her mother still had that gentle smile and those soft grey eyes looked at Elizabeth tenderly.

"Well lass you've got your own way. You've your family here at last. I canna say I'm sorry to leave the ship. What a terrible thing it is to be seasick. I spent days on ma bed in the cabin with ma stomach heaving and then vomiting. I couldna eat anything. Well, I was thankful to have Janet and Fay to help me. All I could keep down was water and I felt so hungry but the doctor warned me not to eat anything. I never want to go through that again, but I wasna alone. I ken half the passengers were sick too."

"I know well how you must have felt. I was sea sick for days and I never want to feel as ill as that again," Elizabeth replied.

She put her arms around her mother and she could not help weeping with joy as they hugged each other and kissed each other's cheeks. When Elizabeth stepped away from her mother she saw that Anne's eyes were wet with tears also. The words her mother had spoken in her rich Scottish accent meant more to Elizabeth than any word she had heard since she had been in Melbourne.

Robert, Janet and Fay were laughing and each stepped forward and shared in the warm welcome from Elizabeth. Fay was now twenty-one, and Janet seventeen. What a change she saw in her sisters. They had been working at the linen factory, mixing with so many women, earning their own wage, and she could see the maturity and confidence in their faces.

Fay had her light brown hair in the new bobbed style and she was wearing much more makeup around her eyes than Elizabeth had ever used. She was slender with a pale smooth complexion with a tinge of rouge on the cheek. She wore a loose silk shift type dress with stylish twenties style shoes. Janet had copied her sister with her hairstyle but her hair was black, and her pale Scottish skin highlighted her soft pink lipstick. Elizabeth could see that Janet would have no difficulty in attracting young men when she settled into their home in Burnley.

Elizabeth had waited and planned for this moment, and now that her family were beside her she knew that life would be different, and filled with new hope for all of them.

.o0o.

CHAPTER 15: Edward

The Morgan brothers Edward and Llewellyn and their friend Dick Jones finally disembarked from the migrant ship the *S.S. Borda* in November 1925. Twenty-five year old Edward was over six feet tall with sandy coloured curly hair receding from his forehead, blue eyes and generous full lips. He was powerfully built, with a broad muscled back, rich olive smooth skin and very large hands.

Llewellyn was very different from his brother in appearance as he had dark thick hair, brown eyes and thin lips. He was about five feet nine but was also well muscled and looked very fit. Llewellyn was now twenty-seven. He had left the village of Llangadfon in Wales, hoping to find a future in Australia with the thought of one day bringing out Meggan, a Welsh girl whom he loved deeply.

Llewellyn had been courting Meggan for a year and planned to marry her. However her father, who owned a prosperous farm in the Foel Valley, had said that he would never be permitted to marry her as he was so poor. Llewellyn was determined that he would one day prove that man wrong and make his fortune in Australia.

Their friend Dick was lean and handsome, with a sparkle around his eyes. Like Edward, he was twenty-five years old. The two brothers had grown up with Dick since they were young boys.

Edward and Llewellyn's parents had died of tuberculosis. They were tenant farmers and lived in a small stone cottage on the farm. Their mother died in 1908 and their father two years later. They were cared for in the cottage by their grandmother. After she died the two boys were taken to live with their uncle on his farm.

They all went to the small rural school in the Foel Valley in Mid Wales. At the end of their final year in primary school all three boys left school to work on relatives' farms.

Dick's aunt raised him in the village, as his parents had died of tuberculosis when he was seven. He spent much of his time wandering across the valley, often missing school for days. His aunt had little control over Dick, but she was kind and always made sure he had food, shoes and decent clothing.

The villagers regarded Dick as an uncontrollable rascal but his friends Edward and Llewellyn enjoyed being around him. He encouraged them into many escapades, often leading the brothers into trouble, culminating in a belting with a thick leather strap from their uncle.

As teenagers, their misdemeanours included smoking behind the barn, stealing bottles of home-brewed beer from the pantry and arriving back into their uncle's place with slurred speech and almost drunk. There were others. It was Dick who usually was the leader of the group, but the two brothers were keen participants as well.

Dick was popular with the girls in the village, and it was rumoured that he had fathered at least two children in his early twenties. The brothers knew that it was the main reason Dick was keen to leave Llangadfon. He did not want to be tied down in poverty and in marriage, in that small village.

By the time they were in their twenties, their bodies were hardened with the strenuous work they had to do working out in the fields most of the year, especially through the harsh long winters of mid Wales.

Dick Jones had talked of migrating for the past three years and finally convinced the Morgan brothers to go with him. Dick, Llewellyn and Edward decided to migrate together and leave Llangadfon as they all felt trapped in the grind of their labour on their relatives' farms with no hope of leaving the valley. It was the migration scheme that they had read about that gave them hope of finally breaking away from their life on the farms.

"There's no hope of any future in this place lads. We have no chance of having our own piece of land. It has been farmed by the same families for generations," Dick had explained. "I heard that Australia is the place to go. Land grants are even being offered to some migrants there I hear."

The three men were the first to ever leave their village to emigrate. It caused much discussion among the farmers. The brothers had worked on their Uncle David's farm since leaving school. He had paid them a pittance of less than a pound a week, and there was no hope of ever saving any money. David was to lose his two cheap workers, so naturally he was very upset at their momentous decision.

David's daughter Blodwyn was fourteen and she adored her cousin Edward. He wrote poetry in Welsh and they shared a love of singing the Welsh hymns they had learnt at Chapel. She had imagined one day marrying him, but knew it was just a dream.

Blodwyn handed Edward her Welsh Bible as he was leaving her home and said, "Always keep it with you and never forget our Welsh language." She sobbed and hugged Edward tightly, saying, "You will always be in my thoughts and one day you might return to visit us."

Edward knew that it was his cousin Blodwyn he would miss most, but in his heart he realised he would never see her again.

The ship '*Borda*' was a twin screw steamer of 1200 tonnage and carried just over one thousand passengers, mainly families and single men. The majority of the passengers were migrants heading to Melbourne and Sydney. It left Tilbury Docks in late September carrying the hopes of the hundreds of migrants heading towards their new lives in Australia. How could Edward ever imagine that his future wife Elizabeth would embark from the same dock two years later?

The three men had travelled via the Cape of Good Hope in third class. It had been a struggle to find the fare of seventy pounds, even though they were classed as assisted migrants. The Commonwealth Government was keen to attract young single men to the migrant program as there was a huge shortage of agricultural workers in Australia. The three men were therefore ideal candidates for the migration program to Australia.

After disembarking from the *S.S. Borda* early in December, they headed out of Melbourne on a fruit pickers' train to Mildura. The government had arranged their work and accommodation, picking grapes on a one hundred acre fruit block just out of Mildura.

Their pay was to be thirteen shillings a day, which was a good rate then, and the owners of the fruit blocks were desperate for workers to help with the harvest.

The train was very crowded and the hard benches and sleeping areas were very uncomfortable for the journey to Mildura. At the stations on the way the men tumbled out of the hot, airless carriages desperate for a little food and drink. What a relief it was to finally stand on the platform at Mildura, after fifteen hours in such cramped conditions, with the sweaty unwashed bodies of the men fouling the air around them in the carriage.

Wales to all three of them was still a precious part of their memories as they had left family and friends behind. However after the journey out on the ship, the harshness of the dry dusty landscape that confronted them as they looked out of the train window made their life in Wales seem utterly remote now. They knew that there was little hope of ever returning. What was the their future back in their village? Their parents were dead and they were all working and living with relatives, with no hope of ever owning their own farms.

The picking season in Mildura lasted three months and the men were formed into gangs. The work was hard as on many days the temperature in the afternoons reached well over one hundred degrees. His grape picking gang gave Edward Morgan the nickname of 'Big Ned' as he was the strongest man on the fruit block. His olive skin was soon tanned to a rich honey colour from working in the blazing heat picking the fruit. He always wore a hat and was lucky that he did not get sunburnt. Some of the gang with their freckled pale complexions were suffering constantly with sun burnt lips and noses.

On the second day of picking one of the gang sidled up to Edward and said, "It's bloody good money mate, but you'll have to work like a bloody navvie to earn it. You'll be lucky to last a season in this heat."

After a week of picking Edward did wonder whether indeed he would last a season, but he was determined that he would save and at least see out the three months.

The accommodation was crude, consisting of a long shed with canvas stretchers topped with thin straw mattresses. There were two water tanks outside, with troughs for washing and outside cold showers set up nearby surrounded by some canvas. The food supplied was adequate, but it was mainly mutton, potatoes and some green vegetables. However there were plenty of grapes and dried sultanas to eat for a sweet.

A comradeship developed among the various gangs that worked on the blocks. Edward and Dick met Malcolm, an Australian who helped them to understand the 'Aussie' slang words that the gangs used in their speech so naturally. Malcolm was impressed by the brothers' willingness to work in the heat, keeping up with his mates in the gang.

He said to Edward, "Youse are bloody good workers and will soon become real Aussies. I'm gunna be your mate and teach youse some of our lingo."

The fruit gangs spent much of their free time drinking at the Working Mans Club in Mildura, and Malcolm first took Edward, Llewellyn and Dick there. They had never seen such a long bar. At 299 feet, it was advertised as the longest in the Southern Hemisphere, with men lined to four deep, swilling down icy cold glasses of beer. How different this was to the small pubs in the villages of Wales serving pots of warm British beer. It did not take many trips into Mildura for the three men to get the taste for the Aussie cold beer. After the long hot days bending over the grape vines, it was a trip they all looked forward to, as well as sharing plenty of yarns with other pickers at The Club.

The blocks were irrigated and the rich green of the vines were a great contrast to the unirrigated reddish brown dry dusty land surrounding the blocks. Almost eighty per cent of the migrants were chasing the extra 'quid' hoping to set themselves up as owners of a small block, or to head back to the city to find better work.

At the end of the picking season Ned, Llew and Dick decided to head north to the cane fields of Queensland. They had formed friendships with some of the other pickers who had been working on the fields there the previous cane cutting season. One of the pickers, David, had worked on the cane fields near Mackay and he had persuaded the three men that there were more opportunities to own land there. It was cheap and the Government was keen for farmers to grow more sugar.

"Well mates," he said, "I reckon it can't be worse than the conditions we have here and you'll earn more pay than here. I heard the Government is pouring money into the development of primary industry and the sugar industry is booming. The Government is protecting the sugar industry and it is the place we should head for."

.o0o.

CHAPTER 16: Four Years Later

The strong harsh sun of Northern Queensland seemed to have sunk into every pore of Ned's huge muscled body over the past four years. His hands had become gnarled and calloused from the backbreaking work in the cane fields. His entire body was coated in a rich dark tan. Edward's fair, curly hair had receded further from his forehead and had bleached to the colour of dry parched yellow grass.

At the end of each cane cutting season in Mackay, Edward, Dick and some of the other men headed back to Mildura as they knew they would easily find work there. It was hard to find employment all year in Mackay as it was the start of the Depression that was sweeping across Australia and forcing so many out of work. The fruit blocks around Mildura still needed workers and the men knew that they would easily find jobs as pickers there.

The wide brown parched lands of northern Victoria, and the rich tropical growth of the northern Queensland cane growing areas, both contrasted sharply with Edward's memories of the high mountains and green valleys of mid Wales. The biggest difference was the space and vastness of their new country compared with the small green valleys and villages of Montgomeryshire in Wales.

Each of the three men had known every neighbour living on their farms in the Valley. They could name every crag they had climbed and they had explored every hill surrounding their village. Families had lived in the same village for generation upon generation, had ploughed the same fields. The grey basalt houses of the village had weathered the test of time for generations also and many had stood for more than a hundred years.

The graveyard near Edward's village contained the bodies of his parents, grandparents and great grandparents and other close relatives. Edward did feel a longing at times for Wales, but he realised that it was here he had to make his life. However he did wonder if he would ever feel the same about this new adopted country and call himself an Australian.

Edward had seen a change in Llew's and Dick's attitudes. Without realising it, they all had become assimilated to Australian customs and the Aussie slang was becoming part of their vocabulary. Mixing with the rough Aussie bushies and working in the cane fields had changed them. Dick now identified himself to others as an Aussie. Their Welsh accents had also changed somewhat to an Australian drawl.

They all saw the opportunities available as the area around Mackay was bursting with growth, with the cane fields expanding to the north and west of the town, but it was Llewellyn who took the gamble to stay and buy a small cane farm.

The work in the cane fields was hard on the men's bodies but they had become accustomed to the life, and their bodies now were very fit and toughened to the work.

The cane fields were always burnt before the cutting of the cane. The cane fires burnt fiercely, with thick smoke and ash filling the air, polluting all the surrounding area. The men's bodies were black with the ash as they sweated profusely, their muscles aching from handling the heavy cane knives, and then lifting the cane in bundles onto the trucks. The motions of cutting, stacking, and loading became so automatic that they drained all thought from a man's head.

After a shower and some grub, the men would head into Mackay and fill their bellies full of cold thirst quenching beer, that never seemed to quench the thirst at all.

The second year in Mackay, Llew borrowed two hundred pounds from his brother Edward and bought a small farm in shares with another mate. It had a small Queenslander-style house on the farm that Edward and Llewellyn moved into. They worked to renovate it and paint it for Llew's future bride.

Llew had a desperate urge to settle permanently in Mackay and establish his own farm. He saw the opportunity that he would never have had in Wales. Llewellyn had been writing to Meggan telling her of his plans for over a year. He knew that she was very fond of him and now she was in her early twenties, Meggan could break away from her father's control if he could pay her fare out and provide a home for her.

He was sure he could persuade her out to join him as his fiancée, and become his wife. He would prove to her parents that he now owned a cane farm and would one day perhaps be a wealthy sugar cane farmer. Llewellyn paid for Meggan's fare at the end of his third year, as he wanted her to be coming to Australia as his future wife and not as a migrant.

Llewellyn Morgan could never have imagined that by the end of the 1950s he would have become one of the wealthiest sugar farmers in North Queensland, owning several cane farms around the district, stretching up into the Burdekin area, and even branching out into cattle farming.

Edward decided that this fourth year in Mildura was to be his last. He had heard Dick had managed to save enough to buy a small fruit block not far from Mildura. His boyhood friend had met an Australian girl the previous year and was considering marrying her, but was still undecided, as he also had promised to marry a lass in Mackay the previous year. Edward did not care to meet him again after hearing the news recounted by their old friend Malcolm.

Malcolm had been among their first mates among the pickers of Mildura, and had travelled with them to and from Mackay for work. Bitterly the Aussie told Edward what had happened to destroy his friendship with Dick.

"I thought Dick was a good cobber. We worked as mates for three years and I trusted him. Last year in Mackay, our mate Dick got pretty keen on a local sheila. I'd got paid a month's wages and I bought meself a beaut dark blue suit that cost me twenty quid."

Malcolm shook his head at the thought, and continued. "My mate Dick came back to the camp that night and said he had to ask his girl to marry him as she thought she was 'up the duff'. The wedding was planned for the following week and as the cane season was almost over, he said he wanted to take the girl down south and settle down for good. He asked me to be best man and I was real pleased to do this job, as we'd become cobbers over the years. He said not to mention it to you, as you might be upset not to be the best man."

Edward was shocked to hear the rest of the tale, but he knew of Dick's past history in Wales.

"Dick said that he hadn't enough loot to splash out on a suit because he needed all of his wages for fares and would I lend him my new suit? We were about the same size and when he tried it on it looked as if it had been made for my mate. He strutted around in front of the mirror just before the wedding and I thought, what a cocky young buck he'd become over the past years."

Edward knew Dick always did have an eye for the girls, and that they were attracted to him with his handsome looks and confident air. He had listened to Dick flirting and flattering the naive young girls who were easily persuaded by his false charm.

Malcolm then continued with his story. "I arrived at the church just before my mate, as his wedding was to be at two o'clock. The car drew up just after two with the bride, a real good-looking sheila, and her old man. They thought Dick was already in the church. We waited and waited till after 3 o'clock. The bride started to cry when she realised the bugger was not going to show up."

"I took her into the small room at the back of the church, with the mother and father tagged along behind. I tell you it's hard to talk to a sheila in that sort of fix. As she cried I said to her, 'Don't worry lass. Think yourself lucky - you've only lost a bastard but I've lost a bloody good suit and that cost me plenty of sweat in the cane fields.' I've never seen Dick since, but after what that rotten bastard did to me, and to that girl, I don't trust anyone except myself. If I ever catch up with him again, he'll cop a punch in the snout."

Edward had not seen Dick since he had left Mackay and headed back south. He was very hurt and angry at the callous way Dick had treated both his 'fiancée', and their friend Malcolm who was their first real Aussie mate. Dick and Ned had teamed up with Malcolm cutting the sugar cane in Mackay, and working in the pickers' gang on the fruit block in Victoria when they had first arrived there from Melbourne. Such seemingly casual betrayal deeply disappointed Edward, who was at heart a very decent, loyal man.

.o0o.

CHAPTER 17: When Edward Met Elizabeth

Edward slumped in a chair in Mildura and pondered his future. 'What will I do now? My mates are finding women to settle down with. I've not managed to do the same.'

The pickers' train was heading back to Melbourne in a few days as it was nearing the end of the grape harvest. The grapes were almost finished and as he looked across at the green leaves rapidly browning in the hot sun he made his decision.

"It's Melbourne I'll head to also," he told himself.

Edward's memory of the city was vague, as he had not had the chance to explore any of it. He had travelled through on the pickers' train from the ship four years ago without spending any time there. All he had seen was a blur of rooflines of the suburbs through the train windows.

"Melbourne is the place I started out from, and it's to the city I'll go, to try to find my future."

It was March 1930 when Edward arrived at Spencer Street Station. He had a strange feeling that as the train approached the city he was travelling back through time. It had been four years ago when he had stepped off the gangway of the *S.S. Borda* with his brother and Dick and headed north. The years had gone quickly and what had he really achieved? Here he was back where he had started.

The train journey had taken about fifteen hours but Edward had the ability to relax almost anywhere and doze off. He had sprawled his large frame out across the wooden bench seat and drifted into a half sleep, dulled by the regular rhythm of the train wheels.

Edward did know that he had changed. He was identifying himself more and more with the sense of being an Australian. Throughout the trip he had hardly noticed the scenery altering gradually from the stumpy Mallee scrub and dry red soil to the brown grazing lands of Central Victoria. The gum trees had become taller as the train rocked closer to Melbourne, and then there were the iron rooftops of the houses as it travelled into the suburbs.

Edward pulled himself into an upright position and rubbed his eyes. It was less than an hour before the train would slide into Spencer Street and disgorge its passengers. He looked out of the window and was shocked at the expanse of the suburbs and the industries close to the city.

'I've got to get things sorted out here and have a plan for the next few weeks. Surely I'll find a good permanent job here, and maybe get married one day,' he thought.

The Welsh-born immigrant knew that he was now on his own. His brother was settled on his cane block out of Mackay and he did not care where Dick had finally settled. He felt alone. There was no one he knew in Melbourne to share his thoughts with.

One of the pickers had given Edward the address of a guesthouse in St. Kilda and he pulled the crumpled piece of paper from his wallet.

"Well, I'll head there first. I can't drift forever. Everyone needs a place to go to, a bed to sleep on and regular meals. This place will do for a start."

Edward stood on the edge of the footpath outside Spencer Street Station with his battered cardboard suitcase clutched in his large brawny hand. He shivered as the cold damp air seeped through his thin jacket and trousers. It was late April and the Melbourne skyline in the dusk was filled with thick, dark clouds. It was cold, and the passing cars' wheels were splashing water onto his trousers. The rain was now falling steadily in a solid stream.

The big cane cutter shivered and thought, 'I'll have to get some decent warm clothes down here.'

Spending the summers around Mildura and the winters in Northern Queensland meant that he hadn't needed to bother with real winter clothing.

The collar of his open necked shirt was soaked, and rain drips were running down his neck. Luckily a taxi was parked at the kerb side, and Edward leaned into the driver's window.

"Where to, mate?" asked the driver.

The effort to find his own way to St. Kilda seemed too great, and Edward gratefully handed the slip of paper to the driver. He sat in front seat of the taxi, lifting his case over to the back seat.

"It's a bloody foul night mate, but it is good for my business," remarked the cabbie. "It's not far to St. Kilda and I know that place you're staying at. It has good digs."

Edward was too tired to talk and was thankful to just lean back against the seat and let someone else take him to his destination.

The guesthouse was a brown weatherboard home in Princes Street, St. Kilda. It had a wide front veranda with a picket fence and a pocket sized front yard. He rapped on the brass handle of the door and the landlady opened it. Edward's clothes were damp and it was obvious he was cold and weary from his long trip.

"Hello, my name is Edward Morgan and my mate in Mildura gave me your address and said that you might have some lodgings for me till I find my feet. I've just come from Mildura on the train. He stayed with you last year. His name is David. I don't know anyone in Melbourne but I hope to get a job here soon." The words tumbled out in a tired torrent.

Grace the landlady looked at the tall blue-eyed man standing in front of her. She was taken with his gentle voice with just a touch of an accent, and his warm smile.

She took hold of his arm and in her strong Australian accent said, "Well I did like David, and if he gave you this address then that is a pretty good reference for me. I do happen to have a spare room. There are four other blokes here from the country and two have found jobs already."

The new tenant walked down the centre passage and was shown into his bedroom. It was clean and neat with a hand basin, a small table and chair. A woollen rug was on the floor near the single bed. After the rough 'digs' Edward had put up with for years he thought this was just luxury.

"Well, how will this suit you, Edward? Two pound ten shillings a week I charge," said Grace, the owner of his new home.

He could hardly speak, he was so thankful to be here and he just longed to rest on that single bed, he was so tired.

"Thank you Grace, and I'm happy to help you around the house if you need it?"

Grace smiled, as she knew that Edward would be a good boarder and she'd have no trouble with him. "Welcome to my home Edward, and you can stay till you get sorted out with a job."

At breakfast and in the evenings Edward did enjoy the company of his grey haired landlady. She was in her mid fifties. She was plump with very a generous bust, which seemed to want to burst from the buttons of her blouse. Grace was generous with the food, joked often with the men and made time to listen to their problems at meal times.

Her raucous Australian accent rang through the house calling the men to breakfast in the mornings. It gave each of the men a feeling of being welcome as they were greeted with her cheerful smile. The smell of fried bacon, eggs, plenty of toast with butter, and her home made marmalade was plenty of incentive to get to the breakfast table at seven o'clock each morning.

It was hard to walk out of the guesthouse each morning searching for work. Edward scanned the newspapers, searching the 'Situations Vacant' columns of the *Age* and *Herald* newspapers daily. Grace had the newspapers delivered and she made sure Edward had the chance to scour the columns each day.

He was looking for sales or labouring jobs, as he knew that without any formal qualifications that was all he could hope for. Each job that looked promising, he circled in the paper. He then tried to get to the appropriate place early in the mornings, but he was always too late. Men were always there before him. He was sure that those fellows queued outside the newspaper printing offices, scanning the papers well before dawn, so as to be first in line for any job that was offering.

It was a tough time in Melbourne, as the headlines in the papers were constantly writing about the disastrous effects of the Depression that were causing so many businesses to fold. He read how tough the banks were now making it for businesses to borrow. Edward thought that once again he would miss his chance to find permanent work.

It was now three weeks since Edward had landed back in Melbourne. Three weeks of precious time where each day that passed made him more miserable.

Edward still had over two hundred pounds saved from his cane cutting and picker's wages, but that would only last out another few months. He thought about his mate John, a dark skinned Australian. They had become friends at Grace's guesthouse. John had been trying to get Edward to go into partnership with him in a used car lot that was going cheaply for rent in St. Kilda. Edward trusted John and he made this car business sound convincing.

This idea of selling used cars was way outside of anything Edward had ever considered, but after three weeks of exhausting himself chasing after jobs that were never there, he thought, 'I must have a crack at something soon. I am going nowhere at present.'

The car business turned out to be disastrous for Edward. He thought later that he should have had the sense to realize that during a Depression, no one had the cash to buy a car, or could afford to run one. John had talked Edward into the deal by convincing him that this was the time to start a business.

"Cars are selling at rock bottom prices. Get into the trade now, and establish ourselves," John had said.

It had been a fair thought, but it would require patience waiting for conditions to improve. Edward spent a fortnight sitting in the small office in the car yard with John, without a single buyer, but seeing plenty of curious people just wanting to look.

The big Welshman decided he'd had enough. He walked out of the business leaving John his share, and making it John's problem. John was still convinced he would succeed.

Edward thought, 'Perhaps John would make a go of it. He certainly knew how to talk to the customers, and he did have much more money to take that gamble.'

The following week John sold his first car in the yard and made a good profit. He started buying second hand cars very cheaply because families could now not afford to buy petrol. John was sure that his business would succeed if he could manage to last for another few months.

Edward had lost one hundred pounds. He knew though, that he would never make a salesman as he didn't have John's gift of the gab, and was too honest to cheat anyone with a dodgy second hand car.

It was Friday and Edward had now been staying at the guesthouse for four weeks. John convinced Edward to go to the British Isles Club in the City to a dance. He was very reluctant as although he had done some dancing on the ship and had learnt to waltz, he had not tried since.

He dressed carefully, wearing the new suit he had purchased two weeks ago to impress the customers at the car yard. As Edward knotted his tie around his neck, it seemed to almost throttle him. He hated wearing ties, as they seemed designed to choke out his breath. The open necked short light cotton shirts he wore up north suited him much better.

The British Isles Club was crowded and Edward felt very self conscious and awkward as he stood at the edge of the dance floor. He knew he would make a poor dancing partner, and it was an effort to make conversation with these unfamiliar women.

Suddenly across the dance floor he saw her. She wore a pale blue silk dress that clung to her slim hips. Her hair was softly curled around her ears and was as black as coal. It was her face, though, that really caught his eye, with such a pale complexion, and those red full lips and a beautiful smile. He was sure she smiled across at him.

He walked across the room with renewed confidence in his step. 'Please, let her say yes to me,' he thought.

Elizabeth looked up at the tall fair-haired stranger approaching her and as he reached her, he gave her a broad smile. He had a smooth, olive complexion, a strong lean body, blue eyes, a roman nose and generous lips.

"Please can I have this waltz?" he asked. "I'm not much of a dancer but I would like to try."

Elizabeth let herself be drawn into his strong arms as he slowly led her onto the dance floor. She noticed what big hands he had, and he made her feel so small against his chest. Edward was surprised at how he had remembered the waltz movements, but the music had an excellent rhythm to it and Elizabeth had no trouble following his steps.

They spent the rest of the evening together and Edward felt that he did not want to let her disappear from his life. There was a flutter in his chest each time they danced. They had only just met a couple of hours ago, but Edward was certain that he had met the woman he wanted to eventually marry.

Elizabeth enjoyed being with Edward and was also hoping that she would meet this man again.

"Let him ask me home," she whispered to herself.

It was just after eleven when the last dance finished and Edward and Elizabeth stood beside each other. They were both wondering whether they would meet again.

It was Edward who turned toward Elizabeth and shyly asked, "Could I escort you home, please?"

He did not want to take the chance of never seeing her again.

Elizabeth saw Janet and Fay walking towards them and said, "I've come with my sisters and I'm sure they will not mind."

She introduced Edward to her sisters and they all agreed to leave together. Janet and Fay were quietly pleased to see Elizabeth with this striking, tall fair hair man. Since arriving in Melbourne, Elizabeth had been so busy sewing for her clients at Mrs Crosby's home, sewing for her family, and working for the Cowell family three days a week, she had not bothered to go out with her sisters. Furthermore the memory of her last encounter with Richard on the ship still hurt her deeply. She had trusted him, and almost lost her virginity to him.

It was Janet and Fay who had persuaded Elizabeth to come with them that night. They had been to the Club several times and enjoyed meeting the Scottish, English and Irish migrants. The British Isles Club dances meant that they could meet many people who shared many of the problems of finding jobs, meeting the opposite sex, and adjusting to living in Australia.

It was after midnight when Edward arrived back at the guesthouse. He felt light headed, light footed and he wanted to sing and shout and tell the other boarders that he had found his Bess. He had taken Elizabeth back to Burnley and it gave him a chance to chat with the sisters. They were friendly and he enjoyed listening to their banter with each other, but it was Elizabeth he could hardly take his eyes off. The sisters went inside and he very tenderly held Elizabeth in his arms and kissed her. He was surprised when she returned his kiss and looked up at him. She felt so small and vulnerable in his arms.

They arranged to meet on Sunday at St. Kilda Beach and spend the afternoon in the park and perhaps visit the Luna Park funfair. Edward had never been there but John had talked about it, and how popular it was. In keeping with the Luna part of its name, the park had a giant 'Mr Moon' mouth at the entrance. There was a lot of entertainment inside and many

Melbourne families flocked to it every weekend.

On that Sunday Edward spoke to Elizabeth openly of his life in Wales and in Australia; cane cutting, picking grapes and the trouble he was having in Melbourne finding work. He had not been so frank and honest with a woman for years. He had confided to his cousin Blodwyn in Wales but she was only fourteen. There had been one other woman in his life in Wales, but that relationship had been very different to what he hoped the future held with this beautiful Scottish lass.

He told Elizabeth about the Welsh valley where he had been brought up, the death of his parents, and the harsh life living with his uncle, and working for long hours each day on the farm. Memories of his life came flooding back with such clarity. He wanted her to know everything about him. He remembered the last field he had ploughed before leaving; the same field that his father and grandfather had ploughed before him. He told of the small graveyard near the village where generations of his family were buried.

Elizabeth learnt of his grandmother who had raised him till he went to live with his uncle. He told her of the heavy sides of bacon that hung from the rafters of the old farmhouse where he lived, and how as a teenager he had hated helping in the killing of the pigs. All these things he remembered, and somehow it seemed important that he reach out to this woman and tell her of his background.

After that Sunday they saw each other twice a week, and Edward's love for Elizabeth grew stronger and stronger. Edward now called Elizabeth 'Bess' with her permission. This was his special name for her.

He finally proposed to her in September. Elizabeth agreed, and Edward lifted her up into his strong arms, kissed her deeply and said, "My beautiful Bess, you've made me so happy - I promise I will never let you down."

Elizabeth was still driven by the traditional things her upbringing had led her to seek in a relationship. Deep in her heart, Elizabeth was unsure that she loved Edward as deeply as he did her, but he was so gentle. He had never attempted to arouse her sexually, but when he kissed her she did feel such warmth, and had a flutter in her stomach. 'This must be love,' she thought.

They decided to get married in November at the church opposite Burnley Street, and make it just a small family wedding. Edward asked John to be his best man. Elizabeth's mother Anne had encouraged her daughter in the relationship. Edward was smart enough to bring chocolates or biscuits when he visited, but he did get along well with Anne.

Anne was the source of so many of her daughter's attitudes, conscious and otherwise. She said to the bride-to-be, "Well Elizabeth, I ken you have made a bonny choice. That Edward is a good man, and you'll no do better. He'll make a fine father too."

Elizabeth was now almost twenty-seven. Her mother had settled well in Burnley. Robert, Janet and Fay all had steady jobs. John Cowell had kept his word and Robert now worked at the Carlton Brewery in Abbottsford, which was not far from Burnley, and Fay went to work as a domestic for one of the Cowells' friends.

Janet now worked as a tea lady for a large company: *Patterson, Lang and Bruce* in Flinders Lane in Melbourne. She was slim and attractive and it was Elizabeth who encouraged her to apply for a position there. Luckily a Scottish manager who had lived in Dunfermline interviewed her. He had no hesitation in employing this bright young lass with her broad Scottish accent.

Flinders Lane was the busy heart of Melbourne with its large emporiums and multi-storied warehouses in the long narrow thoroughfare. Elizabeth often visited there, as the lane was filled with clothing warehouses and manufacturers of all types: clothing designers, mill suppliers, button and belt makers, Denton Hat Mills, hosiery and corset makers. The lane looked cavernous with tall six storey buildings reaching up on either side. The street itself was often congested with traffic and the alleys and side lanes were often blocked with men lifting boxes in and out of the factories.

Elizabeth now bought most of her dressmaking supplies there, as it was cheaper than Myers and there was such a variety of materials to select from.

Edward had found a job working on a construction site in Richmond during the past four months. He was hired because he was strong and fit, and the work as a builders' labourer lifting heavy loads of building material was very strenuous. But the pay was eight pounds a week with some overtime pay as well. He saved over two hundred pounds and he knew it would be enough to take his Bess back to Mackay.

They had discussed Edward's plan often and he convinced Elizabeth that he would find plenty of work there. His brother Llewellyn had married Meggan and he had written to him - Llewellyn agreed that they could stay with them till they found a place of their own.

Edward missed working on the land and being out in the open air. He thought that they would have a better future in Queensland and hoped that Elizabeth would quickly adjust to the hot climate and lifestyle as well – better than he was adjusting to the cold and to city living.

Little did he realize how foreign Elizabeth would find her existence, living out from Mackay. With her pale Scottish complexion, and without the support of her family she would find that life there would be almost unbearable.

Elizabeth was concerned about the move. Queensland was so far away. The distance from Melbourne to Mackay was more than four times the distance from Edinburgh to London, and that had seemed a world away when she was young.

She would be leaving her family and her small dressmaking business that was giving her the chance to save. She knew nothing about life in North Queensland. Elizabeth liked being close to the city with such good public transport. For Elizabeth it was a big gamble, but Edward was determined to make the move north. He needed her with him and she wanted him close to her.

.o0o.

CHAPTER 18: The Wedding

Elizabeth had spent many sleepless nights during their brief engagement asking herself the same questions over and over. 'Is it fair to marry this wonderful, caring honest man whose blue eyes just shone with love each time they were together?'

Was it wrong to marry Edward, knowing that she was still unsure about how strong her love for him was? She had been so hurt, trusting her feelings with Richard on the journey out to Australia, and then being callously deceived by him and almost raped.

Entering into a lifetime of marriage with Edward was a huge step, especially as it probably meant leaving her family in Melbourne. When would she ever see them again?

She knew how deep Edward's love was for her. He had told her that he never thought he would be so lucky to find the only woman he believed could ever love, here in Melbourne. Edward simply adored Elizabeth, and was longing to marry her, and to proudly introduce her to his brother in Queensland.

As the wedding date drew closer Edward's joy and pleasure grew at the anticipated fulfillment of their marriage, but Elizabeth's anguish deepened. She was still a virgin and half dreaded a repeat of that trauma she had suffered on the *Beltana*.

The bride-to-be purchased several yards of soft, grey satin for her wedding dress. It was the last dress she sewed at Mrs Crosby's home.

Elizabeth had several regular clients whom she had befriended, and they were upset that she was to give up her dressmaking business. Elizabeth invited some of the clients to the wedding and they took great interest in the design of her wedding dress.

She chose a *Vogue* pattern in the latest style. The tight, fitted sleeves finished at the wrist and had satin covered buttons that extended from her wrists half way to the elbow. Elizabeth had also added as an additional feature a soft, flared overlay that was attached at the shoulders and extended to the elbow. The soft cowl collar exposed her pale long neck, and the skirt of the dress flared to expose her slim ankles and her buckled, satin shoes.

Elizabeth wore an embroidered belt around her waist, clipped together with large, silver decorated buckles. A beautiful round silver brooch joined the cowl collar just below her neckline. Elizabeth's black hair curled below the soft grey hat with its small brim turned upwards. Just below her shoulder were pinned two white gardenias. Janet and Fay had fashioned two satin horseshoes with long ribbons in the same material, and they hung from her wrist down to her hips.

The wedding service was held in the small Presbyterian Church in Burnley which Elizabeth's mother attended every Sunday. Her mother, sisters and Robert were thrilled to be there to see Elizabeth marry Edward. They thought he was a 'braw' handsome, kind man and the siblings were sure that he would be a fine husband for their sister.

Edward had asked John to be his best man and he was pleased to accept. They were now good friends as John still lived in the guesthouse with Edward. John was now selling just enough cars to make a small living and he was confident that in couple of years his car yard would be quite profitable.

The Cowells, Mrs Crosby, the Forsyths and some of Elizabeth's clients had also been invited to the wedding. They had become not just clients but friends, chatting with her as she fitted their dresses and costumes. Elizabeth enjoyed meeting these ladies who were willing to divulge so much about their lives to her. She did not mix with them socially and they were confident that Elizabeth would never divulge their gossip and comments about their private lives to anyone else.

After the wedding and prior to their moving north Edward arranged for Elizabeth's Singer sewing machine to be crated up and sent with some of her other goods, especially several lengths of light cotton, silk and rayon, and plenty of coloured thread, buttons, ribbon and lace. There was a wide range of fabric she could purchase in Melbourne and she knew that she would be sewing all of her dresses in Queensland.

As Elizabeth walked down the aisle with her mother, Edward's heart was bursting and he felt so proud of her. She was truly beautiful in her wedding dress. She looked up at Edward and he held her hand. Her eyes shone and she gave him a wonderful smile. He could hardly believe that she soon would be his wife.

The reception was held in the Sunday School hall next to the church. Anne had worked with the Church Women's Committee to organize the food, table settings and flowers and the Committee were also invited to the wedding service. Janet and Fay arranged the flowers in the church and on the tables.

Edward had booked into a small hotel on St. Kilda Esplanade for their wedding night. They were to stay there for two days before catching the coastal steamer to Mackay.

That night he was nervous as he undressed in front of Elizabeth. She had gone into the bathroom and came out wearing a Swiss white cotton nightdress. He could see the outline of her nipples through the fabric. She looked so vulnerable, and shyly climbed into the double bed. The sheets and embroidered pillowslips smelled fresh with just a hint of the perfume of lavender.

Edward looked at his new beautiful wife, so vulnerable and innocent, and remembered his first sexual encounter with Kathleen in 1919 when he was eighteen. She was a Welsh woman from his original village Llangadfon and was eight years older than Edward.

Kathleen went to the village pub about four nights a week as she was bereft, grieving for her husband Trevor. She was lonely, and longed for male company. Trevor was her first love, and their lovemaking had been frequent, and always very passionate. She found the long evenings almost unbearable without him. Trevor had grown up in the Valley and he was respected and liked by the men. They knew they could count on Trevor if they needed help with their cattle, or an extra hand harvesting before a storm broke, which would have ruined their animal feed that they needed for the long winter.

It was Kathleen who taught Edward where to touch a woman to arouse her. The first time that Kathleen had brought Edward to her rented cottage in Llangadfon, they had been drinking pots of beer at the pub. They were enjoying friendly banter with each other, and it was Kathleen's suggestion that he accompany her to her home.

Kathleen had been married for two years before her husband had joined the Welsh Regiment, and left for the Western Front in France in 1916. He was killed in 1917.

Edward had never had sex with a woman before, but when Kathleen first drew him down onto her, she was more than happy with his erection. She had full breasts, and a soft rounded stomach. Her nipples hardened to his touch, and he put his hands onto into her dark, curled pubic hair and felt her wetness beneath it. He had never seen a woman naked before, and was embarrassed when he ejaculated before he had fully penetrated her. Kathleen had been understanding and patient with the nervous young man. Edward still clearly remembered what she had said: "Well lad, I have to give you some lessons about women's bodies. We have our desires too, and sex is much more satisfying when a man understands that."

Edward met Kathleen twice a week for the next six months. He was so grateful to her – then, and years later. She taught him how to arouse her fully, to prolong his ejaculation till she was ready, and to know when she climaxed. It was joyous when they climaxed together. She taught him the excruciating pleasure of oral sex, and how to gently tease her with his tongue until she would gasp in the joy of their lovemaking. They would then lie in each other's arms, spent with exhaustion as their lovemaking often lasted nearly an hour.

He now knew it was lust with Kathleen. They truly fulfilled each other's desires, but it was not love. Edward realized that he was a substitute for her husband's lost love, and often wondered whether it was Trevor that Kathleen was thinking of when they made love. He realized that their affair would not last as Kathleen had spoken plainly to him of her desire to remain in the Valley, and she wanted security in a marriage. Kathleen was hoping to meet a mature man who lived in Montgomeryshire. She had no desire to ever leave Wales and Edward had little prospect of any future owning a farm there.

In 1922 Kathleen married a returned soldier. She was thirty when she moved into her new husband's elderly parents' farmhouse and the following year she gave birth to a beautiful dark haired son. Edward often wondered whether Kathleen did love her new husband, but he knew that she was assured of the security of living on the farm that would eventually be passed onto them.

It was inevitable that a few of these memories would swirl in Edward's head on his wedding night, as he anticipated making love with his new bride for the first time. Edward slid his body under the crisp fresh sheets and kissed Elizabeth gently. Elizabeth opened her mouth slightly and he responded with his tongue. He drew his new bride closer to him and she felt his erection pressing against her thigh. His body was warm, his olive skin smooth and firm. Edward lifted her nightdress up over her head and continued to explore her mouth with his tongue.

Elizabeth's hands then explored down his strong muscled back. Edward gently teased her nipples till he felt them harden. He then kissed both breasts and moved Elizabeth under him. He entered Elizabeth, trying to not thrust too hard into her. As he moved deeper inside her he felt Elizabeth responding to his urgency, but she did feel some hurt and let out a small groan.

She was moist and her hands were moving passionately all over his lower back. Edward's eyes were closed and he was breathing heavily. He thrust further and further into her, and then with a loud groan he stopped moving, and Elizabeth knew he had climaxed.

They lay quietly together holding each other closely. Edward was concerned that he had been too rough and he again kissed her passionately.

Elizabeth looked into Edward's eyes and told him that he was the first man to have had sex with her. He was aware how tight he felt inside her and asked Elizabeth if he had hurt her.

She replied, "Aye, but it was a hurt I wanted, because I never imagined feeling like that with a man."

He was quietly pleased to be the only man in her life and wanted to make love with her again. She did not tell him about Richard, but felt content in Edward's arms with her head on his powerful chest. He knew that he wanted to kiss her clitoris to arouse her to a deep climax, but that would have to wait till they knew each other's bodies and could make love with total confidence, understanding each others needs.

Elizabeth lightly stroked Edward, happy to feel him hardening again under her hand. Softly Elizabeth said, "Yes," as she also felt a wonderful throbbing sensation inside her that she wanted to go on and on. She now felt so secure in his arms.

This time Edward seemed to be in another world as he thrust into her, but Elizabeth wanted Edward now, so much more than the nervous first time. She knew how much Edward loved her, and Elizabeth believed that their lovemaking would get better and better. She felt such an overwhelming completeness with him that it surprised her.

The next day they were in no hurry to leave their room. It was the first time Elizabeth had fully gazed at Edward's nakedness. They showered together with Edward soaping his wife, his hand gently massaging her whole body, causing him to become fully aroused again. Elizabeth smiled up at him and they made love with the warm water flowing over their bodies.

Edward suggested later in the morning that they find their way to Port Melbourne to check out their embarkation point at the docks. The train from Flinders Street took them to the 'Bay Excursion Platform' on Station Pier. It was where Elizabeth had disembarked three years ago and she now was about to leave Port Melbourne for Queensland.

The pier was crowded with people as a ship was about to berth. It reminded Elizabeth of the excitement she felt greeting her family on that same wharf. The large two-storey building had recently been refurbished and it was impressive with a modern waiting room on the second floor for passenger departures and arrivals.

However they found out that they were to leave from Princes Pier, which was adjacent to Station Pier. It was also a major passenger and cargo terminal. This terminal was also modern with all the amenities passengers could need. It had a large waiting room for passengers, and they watched people disembarking from one of the moveable gangways that made it so much safer to board the ships. The building was well designed to cope with large numbers of departing passengers.

Edward was anxious that their departure would be without any worry so he was thankful that they had explored the area and found out where they were to leave from, as it would likely be very crowded on the Pier with new arrivals as well as departing passengers.

On the second night their lovemaking was even more intense, as Elizabeth was much more confident within herself as she trusted Edward completely. He kissed her softly and Elizabeth responded, opening her lips to him. He flicked his tongue across her nipples and felt them harden in his mouth. He then moved down her body kissing her, caressing her and massaging her until Elizabeth cried out with an intensity that she could not control.

Although Edward was finding it nearly impossible not to thrust himself into her, he waited; and it was Elizabeth this time who pulled Edward down onto her. She was experiencing such pleasure, such powerful intense emotion, that her brain blocked out any other thought but the orgasm she was having. He knew she was ready to climax. He thrust powerfully into her, feeling her body pulsating, and he gasped as he reached his orgasm at the same time as he knew Elizabeth had. They lay with their arms clasped tightly around each other. No words needed to be said.

.o0o.

CHAPTER 19: Travelling North

The coastal steamer left Port Melbourne on the third day after the wedding. Remembering her seasickness as she'd come to Australia, Elizabeth had dreaded the journey. But Edward convinced her that it would be much easier than travelling such a long trip by train. They would have uncomfortable bunks and they would have had to change trains at Albury and Brisbane.

The steamer shuddered and vibrated from stem to stern as it made its way up the coast. The heavy seas lashed over the decks and Elizabeth could almost believe that some giant octopus had grabbed the ship and was heaving it backwards and forwards violently, and had it in such a tight grasp that it must surely break in half.

Another wave of sickening nausea raked through her body as she leaned over the bed and retched into the basin. Her stomach would surely turn upside down as wave after wave of vomiting overcame her. Elizabeth had vowed never again to be seasick and yet, Edward had persuaded her that travelling by ship would be better. What was she thinking of? How could she have forgotten how dreadful the last time had been?

Edward was unaffected, but he was very worried about his Bess. He did all he could to try to help her, washing her face, making sure she had liquid most of the time. However once again Elizabeth could not eat at all.

The rough seas lasted till the ship berthed in Sydney for one day, and it did give Elizabeth some relief. The ocean was much calmer as they headed along the coast to Brisbane. Elizabeth was able to venture into the dining area and carefully eat a small meal. She was tired and exhausted, as apart from lack of sleep she had not eaten for three days.

They decided to disembark in Brisbane and catch the train to Mackay. Elizabeth was terrified that she might get seasick again and the long sea journey to Mackay was beyond what she could face.

The steam train left Roma Street for the 1200-mile journey on the North Coast Railway to Mackay and it largely paralleled the coastline. They booked a sleeper carriage. Edward's large frame barely fitted onto the top bunk, and his head was only about a foot from the ceiling. The cabin had a tiny basin and the toilet was along the corridor, which was very narrow, making it difficult to pass another passenger easily. The train travelled on a 3 feet 6 inch narrow gauge line, and as it rocked and swayed, the rhythm of the wheels made Elizabeth very drowsy.

After the horror of her seasickness on the ship, she was relieved to be finishing the last part of their trip to Mackay by train. They had brief stops at Maryborough and Rockhampton for meals in stations that had cafeterias providing drinks and food.

The humidity at the stations was extreme and it shocked Elizabeth. She had never experienced this sort of climate and her blouse was wet with perspiration. Edward assured her that the humidity only lasted for a few months and the North Queensland houses were built for the climate with wide verandas, window shutters and the living areas set high above the ground level, sitting on high pole stumps. He said it was cool underneath the main house. He did not mention the frogs, insects, and occasional snake that appeared there as well.

The long train trip was about thirty-six hours and it had sucked the energy out of Elizabeth. During the night she listened to the rattling rhythm of the wheels, her thoughts whirling about her head, wondering why she had consented to travel this far from her family, and feeling fearful of what was ahead of her. Elizabeth listened to Edward's deep contented snores coming from above her, matching the rhythm of the train wheels. He was heading back to his brother and the farm life he loved. How different his dreams were to hers.

It had been almost impossible for her to sleep on the narrow bunks, and again and again Elizabeth gazed out at the lush tropical growth. It contrasted vividly with the conditions she'd come to know in Australia - dry hot summers, autumn with the rich colours of the leaves turning from gold to brown, and the frosts in winter. Spring in Melbourne was her favourite season, with the fresh green leaves bursting out from the elms, the blossom on the fruit trees, and the wonderful bird life among the trees in the Cowell's huge garden. She had enjoyed her time in suburban Melbourne, with her dressmaking business and especially being near her family. She had become accustomed to her life there.

The new Mrs Morgan knew that was too late now to change her mind. Her future was with Edward.

For the first time in months Elizabeth also felt nostalgic for Scotland with its cool climate, the beautiful city of Dunfermline and even the small harbour of Dysart. When one was so far from familiar places, it was easy to forget all the misery and poverty of the mining villages, and the icy winters with slushy grey snow hardening into slippery dangerous ice on the roads and footpaths, making walking to work treacherous.

She realized that it was the worry about her new life on a cane farm, meeting Edward's relatives that gave her thoughts of her life in Scotland. She knew that she would never return there again, but there was every possibility she would return to Melbourne one day.

The new bride looked into Edward's blue eyes and honest face as they sat beside each other. Listening to his slow reassuring voice with just a hint of Welsh accent, she was reassured that they would have a good life together. She loved him deeply and he adored her. Would that be enough to withstand the problems they were likely to face establishing themselves here in Queensland?

The porter's voice carried along the narrow passage, calling, "Mackay coming up in fifteen minutes. There will be a half hour stop. Passengers disembarking, please collect your luggage from the end carriage."

"This is it, Bess. I know it's been a long rough trip, but it won't take long for my girl to get over it. Just for me, give this place a chance. I know it's strange and different but I've met some wonderful people here over the past four seasons and you'll get to know them all soon. I know they all want to meet you."

Edward desperately wanted his Bess to grow to love it here. Melbourne gave him his precious Bess, and his heart swelled with pride at the thought that she was now his wife and lover. That trip to Melbourne was a visit he would never ever regret, but during all those months in Melbourne the urge to head north had grown ever stronger within him.

Unlike Elizabeth he disliked the Melbourne climate with its months of cold frosty mornings. It had been an effort to get up so early and work on the building site in the miserable wet weather over the winter months, his body aching with the cold.

Edward was sure he could make a success growing cane, and he had no desire to return to Wales. He knew Bess was anxious about leaving Melbourne, but he hoped that living here, she would come to love this part of Australia as he did, and that they would have the chance raise their family on a prosperous cane farm one day.

Llewellyn and Meggan were to meet them at the station and drive them back to their farm. They were to spend a few nights with them before heading out to a small Queenslander home on a cane farm.

Llewellyn had arranged for Edward to work on the Capes' cane farm. He had worked for the owner, Mr Capes, who wished to retire back in Mackay. The Capes family owned three cane farms and their two sons were kept busy managing those properties.

The jerking of the train as it pulled into Mackay Station quickly brought their thoughts back to the present. Elizabeth was tense as she picked up her overnight bag and book from the seat.

"I know that my brother and Meggan are looking forward to meeting my special girl," said Edward. "I saw Llew standing with Meggan over near the entrance gate. It's almost five years since I last saw Meg in Wales and two years since Llew and I parted. It's going to be good to talk about old times and plan our life here, Bess." He paused and looked at his nervous wife. "Buck up Bess. I know they will like you, because you're my wife."

Edward's strong hands gripped Elizabeth tightly around the waist and it did reassure her as they strode along the station towards his brother and sister-in-law. Bess wondered to herself, 'What was Meggan really like?'

Llewellyn's wide friendly smile, his blue eyes, light brown hair receding from his forehead and his dark tanned olive skin was a reassuring sight. Elizabeth saw in his face much likeness to his brother. She thought, 'Well after all they are kin, so his brother would have some of Edward's characteristics, and hopefully have his kind, gentle nature as well.'

Llewellyn hugged Edward and stepped away saying, "Welcome back brother! So this is the beautiful Bess you've been writing to us about. We've been reading so much about you in Edward's letters, and we're thankful he's decided to come here and settle down with his wonderful Bess."

Llewellyn then took both her hands into his large, calloused hands, looking directly into her eyes and spoke softly to her. "I know that it's not easy to leave your family and move so far from them, but you can count on our support while you sort yourself out here."

Elizabeth looked across at Meggan and noticed that her face did not convey the same warmth in her greeting as Llewellyn as had shown. It was not a friendly, kind look and Elizabeth had an instinctive feeling that she and Meggan would never get along together if they lived together under the one roof.

Meggan's dark brown hair was drawn back into a bun, giving her face a severe look. Her mouth was small and her lips narrow. Her eyes were hazel but the creases that lined the edges of her eyes and at the edge of her mouth gave her face a severe appearance. Meggan was just over five feet tall with generous hips and a plump stomach. Instinctively Elizabeth thought that it was just as well that Llewellyn had arranged a place of their own and they would just be staying for a week with them.

He had also made sure the old farmhouse was furnished. He had collected most of it from the second hand furniture shops in Mackay. Meg had also sorted many of her kitchen cooking utensils, crockery, bedding and towels at Llewellyn's request.

At least the newlyweds would not be going into their new adventure completely unsupported and without some basic essentials and a few comforts.

.o0o.

CHAPTER 20: Arriving In Mackay

The sugar market had suffered in the early twenties because of some bad seasons. However Llewellyn Morgan had enjoyed three years of bumper cane harvests, and the sugar industry was now rapidly expanding. He knew that the Government prohibited the importation of sugar from 1923, and he was now guaranteed a fixed price for his cane. Sugar prices were high in Australia but raw sugar exported to the United Kingdom was sold cheaply, as it was cross-subsidized by the high price paid for it in Australia.

It was the Australian consumer who had to bear the high cost in order for sugar cane farmers like Llewellyn to flourish, but that did not concern him. Many small farmers were now growing sugar all along the coastal strips in North Queensland to take advantage of the fixed prices for which they could wholesale their cane to the '*Colonial Sugar Refinery*'.

As long as the Government maintained the high prices of sugar for consumers and manufacturers in Australia Llewellyn knew he would become very prosperous in future years. He was now considering buying more land to grow cane in the next few years as he realized what a wonderful opportunity he had while properties were much cheaper because of the Depression. The banks were forcing people to sell, as they were not prepared to allow farmers in debt to borrow against their farms.

Meggan's cool, formal welcome had been a disappointment for Elizabeth as she did wish to reach out and be a friend to her sister-in-law. She knew that another woman's company would be important to her; to talk and share opinions, even recipes and problems she would encounter that might seem mundane to her husband. It would be good to have a friend to confide in about personal issues, that perhaps she would not discuss openly with Edward.

They collected their luggage from the end carriage of the train and drove out towards Meg and Llew's home. He had insisted that he be just called Llew and his wife Meg. Elizabeth felt uncomfortable at using their shortened names, but Edward said that he had always called his brother and sister-in-law by those names. She however certainly did not want Edward's relatives to call her Bess. That was Edward's special name for her.

Elizabeth sat quietly as she gazed out at the lush green cane fields stretching into the distance. The sun was hot and Elizabeth's cotton dress clung to her perspiring body. She longed to stand under a cool shower and wash away the stickiness and the saltiness she could feel on her skin. She reached out and clutched Edward's hand as he spoke to her.

"So, Bess, what do you think of this land? It's a far cry from the crowded stuffiness of the city. This is where a man can find his place."

Edward sounded so happy and pleased to be back here that she just smiled up at him, although she knew it was going to be difficult for her to adjust to this strange new life she would now have.

The car turned into the long driveway and Elizabeth was impressed with the tall cream painted Queenslander home with its green shutters looming up in front of her. The walls were weatherboard with a corrugated iron high roofline. Edward had talked about the different style of homes in North Queensland, which were well suited to the tropical climate, and this one was impressive in size. There were wide wooden steps leading up to the main house and the bottom area was partially surrounded by wooden trelliswork.

Tall coconut palms lined either side of the driveway. The garden area had many colourful plants and shrubs as well as other exotic palms. She had never before seen plants and shrubs that were so bright in colour and variety. There were banana palms, orange trees, paw-paw and mango trees giving much shade around the house.

'Meg and Llew must have worked very hard to purchase this property,' she thought. 'No wonder Edward thought he could make a success of it here too.'

The car was driven into a huge iron shed that also contained a large tractor and truck. There was a long wooden bench at one end of the shed, with enough tools to build a house and maintain all the equipment needed on the farm.

As soon as Elizabeth alighted from the car the heat and humidity were almost unbearable. Never had she experienced a climate like this. Her face became flushed with the heat and she could feel the perspiration dripping down her body underneath her dress. Elizabeth wondered how she could ever tolerate these conditions, especially with her pale Scottish complexion that would burn so easily under this hot sun.

They walked up the front stairs and Elizabeth was impressed with the spaciousness of the home. The large fan was wafting cooling air down onto her as they entered the large living room with an enormous dining table occupying the centre space. A wide veranda ran round the whole of the house perimeter and was partially covered in wire screens. There were shutters that opened out onto that veranda allowing the late afternoon breeze to blow in. The greenery all around the house added to the cool temperature as well.

The four bedrooms were off the living area, using some of the veranda space. Meg showed Edward and Elizabeth into one of the bedrooms. The shutters were open and Elizabeth was pleased to see a large fan turning slowly in the room. Meg and Llew led them down to the large kitchen that was underneath the house, along with the laundry.

Llew remarked, "Most of the Queensland homes here have the kitchen underneath as it's cool and easy to bring in the supplies rather than climbing those stairs. We spend most of the day down here too when we are not out in the cane fields."

Meg had prepared a salad with cold roast beef, but she did not attempt to encourage Elizabeth into much conversation with her. However the meal was excellent. It was the first time Elizabeth had ever tasted fresh mangos, which were served for a sweet, and she said that they were a truly delicious treat.

Meg said, "We have several Bowen mango trees on the property and you are welcome to take as many as you wish. There are plenty of coconuts falling on the ground too."

Edward and Llew stayed up very late that evening talking away the two years that they had been apart. They were laughing and joking about their past life in Wales, and it was clear to Elizabeth when she saw the joy in Edward's eyes that he was thrilled to be back with his brother. However she also could not help but observe that Meg did not look so pleased at

Edward's return to Mackay.

Elizabeth was tired after the long journey, and she was relieved to say, "Goodnight." She sank between the fresh white sheets. The mosquito netting frame that hung around the bed was very necessary. Elizabeth heard the sound of the mosquitos buzzing, and occasionally a moth batting its wings against the netting. She was so exhausted she was not aware of Edward climbing in beside her. She awoke to find Edward lying with his arm clutching her breast and snoring softly beside her.

Although her in-laws had welcomed them into their home, and Llew's wife had prepared a wonderful Queensland salad, Elizabeth was conscious of a coldness in Meg's attitude towards her and she realized it would not be easy to become friends as their personalities were so different.

'Maybe Meg resented Edward's arrival, as it was obvious Llew was excited to have his brother here and intended helping him settle. Perhaps Meg was jealous of her husband's affection toward his brother. Perhaps Meg was worried that Llewellyn was prepared to offer Edward a share in their property.' These thoughts drifted into Elizabeth's head just before she sank into a deep sleep. Unlike her husband, Elizabeth was very unsure whether she could ever make her permanent home here in the tropical north.

.oOo.

CHAPTER 21: A Home In The Canefields

Edward and Bess drove out along the narrow bush road towards their new home. The tall green grasses along the edge of the road almost reached out to touch the sides of the car. The cane fields stretched out to the horizon where some of the land had been recently ploughed, and Bess saw the distant blue haze of the mountain range. The humidity was very high and her face was flushed with the heat.

Edward had explained to Elizabeth that he would be very busy out in the cane fields as the planting season would soon commence, and then once the cane had reached a certain height, the rows would need to be constantly furrowed and weeded. The cane cutting season would start about June and he would work with a gang of Italian workers who the Capes family contracted each year.

The car turned off the road onto a narrow track. Right up to the edge of the track was ploughed ground now ready for planting. Bess saw their home as they drove into the clearing around it and she was taken back at the dilapidated sight of it. The house was a small Queenslander and it was high set on tar coated timber stumps, ten feet above the ground.

Edward said that the tar stopped white ants from attacking the wood. It had a rusted corrugated iron roof. The house looked as if it had once been painted a long time ago but the brown paint now had almost peeled away from the timbers.

The veranda was open at the front of the house with two very worn cane lounge chairs on it. There was no garden surrounding the home, and not a shrub or a palm tree or mango tree to be seen.

Elizabeth was shocked at the sight of what they were to now call their home. She turned towards Edward. Surely he would not think that she could live out here in this isolated place in that dump of a house.

Edward put his arm around his Bess. His eyes glowed with his love for her, and a broad smile spread across his face. He was completely unaware of her thoughts. He had anticipated being here for so long, he believed that Bess would be as thrilled as he was.

"Here we are, Bess! I've wanted to bring you up north to Queensland from the moment we first met. This is where I worked for the Capes family with my mates, and now we have a chance to make a go of it. I'm going to share farm this place, and one day we will have a home like Meg and Llew."

Elizabeth could barely look at Edward as she stared out at the run down house. In her mind, but not aloud she said, 'I ken how much you like it here and I'll try to help. We canna go back to Melbourne now as we've no money. We have nae choice but to stay here.'

They walked towards the front stairs of the home and she noted the worn timbers on the stairs and the rotting rails. There was a front veranda but it did not extend around the house, which was completely clad in weather-boards with small shuttered windows.

Edward's voice again broke through her thoughts as he said, "We used to shack up in that shed over there with the men during the cane season, and this house was where the Capes lived, but it's altered since then. Llew had arranged for some workers to come out and paint the inside and fix up the kitchen for us."

Elizabeth again was amazed at Edward's lack of awareness. He had roughed it during the cane cutting season and grape picking near Mildura. He did not seem to have the faintest grasp of the reality of what she would desire in a home.

Edward opened the door and there was the fresh smell of paint. The inside corridor had been painted a soft cream to lighten up the interior. They walked into the main living area. There was a large wooden table with six chairs in the centre of the lounge dining area. A corridor clad with light wood ran down the centre of the house, with two bedrooms leading off it.

One of the bedrooms had a wooden framed double bed with netting reaching over the bed head. There was a chest of drawers topped with a mirror, and old trunk in the corner. It had obviously come from Wales as it had Meg's name on the on the lid, and Elizabeth thought it would be handy for clothing storage. The bed had been made up with a floral cotton cover over the top.

There were two shutters opening onto the cleared ground. Elizabeth opened the shutters and looked across to the cane fields. She spotted a long corrugated shed with a closed in section at one end. There was a veranda along one side supported by rough wooden posts.

Edward looked out towards the building and said, "That was called the cane barracks where I lived with the other cane cutters. It was rough but we all got along. The Capes hired Italian gangs to work here, as they were bloody hard workers. They shared their food with me too. When the Capes first came here they lived in that cane shed. Then they built this home."

They went back into the large room and walked down the narrow stairs in one corner of the room. The kitchen had been built in underneath, and had a blackened wood fire stove, and a long bench containing the sink and with cupboards underneath. The cupboards had also been painted in cream. There was a rough timber kitchen table with four wooden chairs. A kitchen dresser was opposite the stove and it had an assortment of crockery displayed there.

"It looks as if Llew and Meg have set us up pretty well, Bess. We have a lot to thank them for."

Elizabeth had to agree, as the main part of the house was clean with newly painted walls, and the dark wooden floorboards also had been polished. Maybe, Elizabeth mused, she had judged Meg too harshly.

They stepped out from under the house and Elizabeth spotted what served as the toilet. It had a wooden door but the rest of it was corrugated iron. She walked across and closed the door and saw that it had just a little light coming from the space between the rafters and the roof. Elizabeth looked up towards the roof and there, gloating down at her were several pairs of eyes. An indescribable panic gripped her and her full bladder was forgotten. She came flying out of the door and ran as fast as she could. Elizabeth flung herself into Edward's huge arms and pressed herself into his body sobbing.

"What is it that's upset my girl so much?"

"Those eyes, those eyes, Edward - that were staring down from the rafters!"

Edward's full throated laughter rang out and he held Elizabeth out from his chest.

"My dear Bess - they're only green frogs that have sat in on those rafters every season since I have worked here. They're harmless."

From that day on Elizabeth kept a long stick against the side wall of the outhouse. Every time she went to the toilet she would open the door wide and then bang hard on three sides of the little structure. The green frogs would hop through the open door and disappear into the cane field.

How embarrassed Elizabeth would be if she had heard the comments of the cane workers each time she ventured out to the toilet. Edward had told the men working in the cane fields about his Bess's terror of the frogs.

"There goes Ned's Bess again. I hope she'll never get the runs up here or she will wear herself out banging that stick."

Elizabeth was also frightened when she first encountered the huge cane beetles, some with large black, glistening, horned bodies. They batted against the netting over their bed each night and terrified her. Each night she would cling to Edward's body and he would always turn towards her and kiss her gently.

"It's nothing to worry about. They're harmless," he explained, but his reassurances failed to allay her fear.

Elizabeth wondered, 'How can Edward remain so calm and placid? Surely he must have some inkling of how I feel!'

Over four cutting seasons Edward had adapted to the climate, and he enjoyed the hard, physical labour of the farm work. He loved being outdoors, mixing with the other cane cutters, who were mainly Italians, listening to their jokes and sharing stories of their earlier lives.

Many of the Italians now owned small cane farms. They were migrants leaving Europe, escaping poverty before the war and settling in North Queensland. After the horrors of the war years they came searching for new lives. Italian relatives who had earlier made the move had encouraged many to come, and they were now making a success of their cane farming, as land was cheap.

Most of the cane cutters were Italians from Southern Italy, as well as Sicilians, Yugoslavs and Maltese. Edward had enjoyed the Italian food: mountains of macaroni, large serves of salad covered in oil, plenty of vegetables and bread. It was filling and seemed to keep him very healthy.

What did sadden Edward was the attitude of many people in the city of Mackay when he visited for supplies. He heard the Italians called names, such as 'dreadful dagoes', and 'scum'. A lot of resentment was caused because the locals thought that the migrants were taking jobs from them. Perhaps they resented the Italians working for wages that were lower than the Union rates of pay.

However he knew how hard the Italians worked and the owners probably knew that too. Edward read some of the disparaging articles in the newspapers denigrating the Italian workers. He had heard of many Italians that now owned successful cane farms further north. They had arrived in the early nineteen hundreds - working hard, cutting cane, and finally managing to buy their own small cane farms.

It was now April and Elizabeth had somehow managed to cope with the humidity and heat. She was frightened though, by the violent thunderstorms that occasionally swept across the land creating minor floods and preventing them driving into Mackay for supplies.

She had known rain in Scotland, of course, and plenty of it, but never experienced rain in such mighty sheets. It poured down and turned the ground around the home into a small lake. Sometimes over ten inches would fall in one day, and then high humidity would follow, draining all energy out of her.

Most of the afternoons Elizabeth spent resting, as she found that it was almost impossible to work after wearing herself out with the morning's chores. She would rise just before six o'clock, make a lunch for Edward to have out in the cane field, bake, clean and wash his sweaty, dirty work clothes.

In the laundry, there was a copper and a concrete double trough with a hand wringer attached to the middle of it. Lighting the wood box under the copper, turning the wringer, pushing the heavy trousers, towels and sheets through it, then heaving it all onto the clothes line, and lifting up the wooden prop up under the line took Elizabeth most of the morning. Edward had strung the line under the house and by the time she had hung the basket of washing out, she was perspiring freely.

Elizabeth hated the North Queensland climate but kept her concerns to herself because Edward tried so hard to help her as much as he could.

Edward spent his days out in the cane fields with two of the other Italian workers planting out the cane, and hoeing and weeding between the rows. Some of the cane was now two feet high. The cutting season would probably start in June and last to about December. Edward would need to make sure the Capes had the Italian cane cutting gangs contracted by then. The Capes valued their hard working Italian cutters and at the end of cutting each season, they contracted the gangs for the following year.

Edward was used to the tough work: hand cutting the cane after the field had been burnt to get rid of the trash, bending over swinging a cane knife, picking the stalks up and loading them. It was tough dirty work and he had to watch out for snakes, rats and other vermin. The cane stalks were cut close to the ground and the hook at the end of the blade was used to remove the trash and dead leaves. The cane was piled high between the rows and the tops of the cane cut off.

The first year of cane cutting for Edward had been almost unbearable. His hands were soft and they blistered, but they gradually hardened with callouses. His back ached as he was bending down low to cut the stalks close to the ground. He had to keep up with the Italians as they worked as a team and were paid by the ton of cane cut. The wages were nearly three times as high as labourers in the towns, who earned about five pounds a week. The skilled cane cutters could earn three times that, but to do so they worked long exhausting hours.

The cane was sticky with the sugar syrup, and he was often covered in soot from head to toe because of the burning of the cane that was carried out before cutting it. His cane knife had a wooden handle with a wide steel blade hooked at the end of it. Sometimes the sticky handle slipped down onto his arm, and he had been cut twice. The edge of the blade was keen, but had to be constantly sharpened with a file. He had to get a new one to attach to the wooden handle about every three or four weeks.

One of his Italian gang workers had cut a vein in his wrist and was lucky to survive. Another of his gang had cut his leg to the bone, when the cane knife had slipped from his hand after hitting a rock half buried in the ground. Edward knew that he could sometimes frighten Elizabeth, as he would be completely blackened with the soot and sweat, with only his white teeth showing.

Elizabeth remembered the first day Edward had headed out to the cane fields. It had been a long day without hearing Edward's reassuring voice, and the warmth of his body as he usually stood behind her and kissed her gently on the cheek, with his hands on her breasts to help her overcome her feeling of depression that hung like a heavy cloud over her. Arriving home much later that day Edward had stood at the door. The whites of his eyes shone through the black grime and sweat of his face. His trousers hung below his belly, suspended by a piece of knotted tattered rope. His blue cotton shirt was clinging to his perspiring body, and his arms below his elbows were covered in dirt and sweat.

Edward's white teeth shone through his parched mouth as he smiled and said, "Hello my Scottish lass! Have you a cold drink for your hard working man?"

She had had her back to him as she worked at the sink. Turning at the welcome sound of his voice, Elizabeth dropped the tea towel to the floor and let out a scream of shock - he was barely recognizable as the man she had kissed and clung to in the morning, pleading with him to wait another day before joining the men on the cane fields. She started sobbing and Edward strode across the kitchen and gathered her into his arms.

"I'm sorry Bess, cane work is a tough dirty way for a man to make a living, but there's no other job for me up here, and we'll have to put up with it for now."

After that first day Edward always made sure that after working in the cane field, he showered and changed before he entered the house. He thought, 'Just as well Bess hadn't seen me come back to the cane barracks after cutting the cane all day when it had been burnt. I would have looked so much more frightening then, blackened with the ash and perspiration from the burnt cane.'

.o0o.

CHAPTER 22: The First Child

By the end of May Elizabeth had missed two periods. She was starting to feel nauseous and could not eat much breakfast without vomiting. Edward was working out in the fields early each morning, and he was unaware of how ill she felt.

Finally, at three months pregnant when she was certain of the new life that was growing inside her, Elizabeth told Edward. She broke the news to him after they had intercourse and they were relaxing in each other's arms.

As ever, Edward had been patient and gentle, and he taken time to allow Elizabeth to reach a climax with his lovemaking. She had discovered the joy of oral sex, and it made their lovemaking even more passionate. Edward had taken time to slowly lead his Bess deeper into a total understanding of her body. She could now reach a wonderfully high arousal, and Edward understood, and could feel that her need was as strong as his. By now Elizabeth was deeply in love with Edward and she trusted him fully.

Edward looked at Elizabeth after her 'announcement', and she could tell by the broad smile that spread across his face and wide open blue eyes how thrilled he was. He put his large hand gently on her stomach, leaned across and softly kissed her.

"My beautiful Bess – I've always wanted a family and now we have one on the way. I will always love and care for you and I promise to work hard to give our family a future."

By the time Elizabeth was four months pregnant, she had overcome her morning bouts of vomiting, but she felt tired most of the day and it was a struggle to rise early to do the household chores. Her stomach was starting to slightly swell and she was thankful that the humidity was now gone and the days were much cooler with little rain.

However she did not feel any of the maternal protective instinct towards her unborn baby that her mother's friends in Scotland had spoken about. Perhaps that deep mother love would come with the baby's birth. Elizabeth had helped her mother care for her two sisters Janet and Fay. After working all day cutting patterns, bent over a sewing machine, stitching embroidery and beading onto dresses and costumes, she did not have any desire to have a large family. Her weekends in Scotland had been mostly taken up with cooking, laundry work, and walking her sisters to the harbour.

In Elizabeth's eyes, children involved very many sacrifices to make sure they were well fed, clothed, and cared for with love. She had seen her mother Anne go without so much in order to meet the children's needs. She had noticed sometimes how her mother skimped on her own meals making sure her children did not go hungry.

Anne had only two dresses to wear, and her shoes were lined with cardboard until the soles were totally worn through. It was only when Robert started work at the mines, adding some extra money to their household, that life became easier for her mother. Elizabeth's dressmaking skills also helped, enabling her to provide Anne with two new dresses at last. It was not an experience of motherhood that filled her with optimism.

The cane cutting season stared in late June and Edward was not able to give Elizabeth much help as he was exhausted after eight or nine hours of cutting cane, chopping the top stalks, lifting it and making sure he was keeping up with his gang. Before he showered he would clean the ashes from under the copper and carry enough chopped timber for the wood fire stove.

He was gentle and undemanding of her with their lovemaking, always thinking of his Bess and aware of her swelling belly underneath him. He was so looking forward to becoming a father and sharing with Elizabeth the task of raising their child.

About once a month Edward and Elizabeth visited Meg and Llew. Llew proudly told them that they were expecting their first child in September. Meg was now six months pregnant. It occurred to Elizabeth that Meg's coldness towards her might have been because she had been suffering from morning sickness when they first met, but the situation between them had not improved.

The two brothers were so relaxed with each other, but it was not the same with the sisters-in-law. Meg's parents had owned a substantial farm in mid Wales and they had spoilt their daughter, indulging her with her own pony, riding lessons, private schooling and a generous dowry before she left Wales.

Meg knew Elizabeth's father had died in the coal mines of Scotland, and knew about her work as a domestic in Melbourne. Meg could not imagine cooking and cleaning for another family. It was part of the reason the Welsh woman thought of herself as superior in upbringing to Elizabeth. Her husband Llewellyn was now making his mark in the district and had recently joined the Sugar Board at their local sugar refinery in Pleystowe near Mackay.

Meg's attitude showed in the way she treated Elizabeth, not giving her the opportunity to meet her circle of friends, and never sharing confidences with her. Meg's coolness towards her sister-in-law hurt Elizabeth, but Edward was unaware of Meg's attitude and he enjoyed the times when he was with his brother. Elizabeth kept her thoughts to herself. She did not wish to cause any friction between the Morgan boys.

Elizabeth missed her friends and sisters in Melbourne. She would have loved to share her thoughts with them, especially now she was pregnant. It was a large part of the reason she wished she were back there with them. She often wondered, 'How long will it be before I can travel back there and show them my baby?'

The journey from Melbourne to Mackay had been long and tiring and it would be very difficult to make that journey again with a baby to care for as well. She realized Edward would now not leave the farm as he hoped to one day own one like his brother. She would have to make that long trip by herself sometime in the future.

Edward worried how his Bess would cope with the heat and humidity that was now increasing in October, especially with the new baby due at the end of November. Most of the afternoons Elizabeth rested under the fan in their bedroom reading. Elizabeth loved reading and when they visited Mackay she always spent time at the lending library, or occasionally buying some second hand books.

Her sewing machine and large box of materials and goods had arrived at Mackay Station in mid April. Elizabeth had made herself three bright light cotton wrap around dresses, each with a tie around the waistline. They were cool and perfect to wear with her swelling stomach. Elizabeth enjoyed the peaceful task of sewing and she sewed some cotton shirts for Edward as well.

He loved observing Bess wearing her well cut dresses, and he admired her skill at dressmaking. It was hard to resist the urge to constantly embrace her, and when the baby started moving inside Elizabeth and he could feel its movement, he felt as if his heart would burst with pride and love for her.

Back in late May Edward had been hoeing some ground away from the house as he was planning to grow some vegetables. He heard a terrified scream coming from the kitchen area where he knew Elizabeth would be, as he had set up her sewing machine in a corner of the room. Elizabeth found it much cooler there and the kitchen table was useful for cutting the cotton fabric. He raced inside and there was a large python curled around the top of the sewing machine.

Elizabeth had lifted the lid and was confronted with a snake about eight feet long. Part of its body was hanging down onto the floor. Elizabeth rushed into his arms, hysterical and sobbing with fear.

"I canna stay here, Edward - I am so frightened!"

Edward took Elizabeth outside and held her close as he called out to one of the workers. Quietly he said to his wife, "We will make sure you never have one here again. We have seen a few pythons in the cane fields but they're not venomous."

Edward's comment did nothing to help allay Elizabeth's terror. She did not believe that she would not encounter a snake again, especially a huge python. She knew that they hid in the fields as the rats provided their food source in the cane.

The worker arrived with a cane knife and killed the snake. He brought it outside and held it up above his head. Once again Elizabeth screamed, "Get it away! Get it away!"

From that day, whenever Elizabeth entered the kitchen she always looked around her. Edward had replaced the wire door, as its frame had buckled and the wire netting had holes in it. The new one now fitted firmly into the doorway frame, but Elizabeth still felt very fearful at the thought of ever encountering a snake in the house or kitchen. She never put the wooden lid on the top of her sewing machine again.

She knew that she would never fully adapt to living in North Queensland with its climate, insects and snakes.

Elizabeth was now over eight months pregnant and suffering physically, making it difficult for her to climb up and down the stairs. She felt the pressure of the baby pushing against her bladder, making her feel uncomfortable, and her back ached for most of the day.

She thought out aloud, "Och, I wish ma family were around me to help. I canna ask Edward to be here. We need the money, and he comes back at night so exhausted. I wish we had stayed in Melbourne. I'm sure ma Edward would have found work."

The smoke from the cane fires that were lit every afternoon, spreading smoke and ash close to the house, sometimes made her cough violently. She could hardly drag herself out of bed in the mornings to start the daily housework routine. It was especially hard washing Edward's filthy, blackened work clothes each day, hanging them out, and then finding the clothes were spotted with ash from the cane fires.

It was almost midday on the last day of November, and the humidity and heat were oppressive. Elizabeth's dress was wet with perspiration, as she had just finished hanging out the clothing that Edward had worn the previous day. He had been returning home for months now with his clothing blackened with ash and dirt and stiffened with perspiration.

Each morning Elizabeth had risen at five a.m. to prepare his morning tea and lunch, then commence the daily washing routine.

Elizabeth walked up the stairs early in the afternoon, and she felt a sharp contraction of pain that caused her to stop and gasp. She sat on one of the chairs in the lounge area and about 30 minutes later she felt another contraction.

When Edward arrived back from the fields at sunset he heard Elizabeth call out to him. He quickly showered and dressed in the clean trousers and shirt and raced up the stairs. Elizabeth's contractions were now about fifteen minutes apart.

She had packed her hospital case during the afternoon and Edward drove her into the hospital in Mackay. Each time Elizabeth felt a sharp pain he slowed the car and put his arm around her shoulders.

He reassured her, "We'll be there soon Bess, and it won't be long before we will greet our first child. You are my life, and soon we'll have a beautiful baby to bring up together."

Edward waited outside the maternity ward until the midwife walked out and said, "You might as well go home, as this baby of yours will not be born tonight. Elizabeth is only dilated about a quarter, and as it is her first it will take a while yet."

Twenty-four hours after she had entered the hospital her contractions were now coming every five minutes. The midwife stared down at Elizabeth and said, "You must try not to push yet. Breathe deeply. It is important to try to relax between contractions."

Another crippling contraction seared through her body and Elizabeth felt as if she was being torn apart. She had never experienced pain like this. She cried out and desperately wanted to push as the pain was now excruciating.

The midwife was now standing with the doctor and the mother-to-be heard him say, "One more contraction and then push, I can see the baby's head crowning now."

The pain was now almost unbearable, but with the next contraction Elizabeth felt a tremendous desire to push as hard as she could. She heard the doctor's words, "Push down Elizabeth. It will soon be over. The head is now out and we just need to get the shoulders through."

With one last once of her strength, Elizabeth bore down till all thought was blacked out. Suddenly the pain was gone, and it was such a relief to be free of it. She raised her head and saw a pair of hands holding a dark haired, tiny baby covered in blood. The baby let out its first cry and the midwife wrapped it in some soft cotton and placed it in Elizabeth's arms.

"It's a beautiful girl and you can be proud of yourself. You did very well."

Elizabeth looked into her baby's eyes and an overwhelming sense of peace, pride and love for this helpless little one came over her. She knew that her life in Queensland was now going to be very different, as looking after her little girl would be her first priority each day. As the baby looked up at Elizabeth and she held the tiny hand, she now understood how strong a mother's love could be.

That evening Edward shyly came into the ward. Elizabeth had showered, washed her hair, and was wearing the nightdress she had worn on the first night of their honeymoon. Edward's eyes glowed as he walked across to her and kissed her softly. The baby was sound asleep in the wire bassinet beside the bed.

He looked down at her and said, "She has your black hair, but she is so tiny. I'll be too frightened to hold her with my big hands. What shall we name our little one?"

"I would like to call her Winifred after your mother."

"Let's call her Winifred Anne as that includes your mother's name."

It was a week later when Edward collected his Bess and Winifred from the hospital. Winifred Anne Morgan had weighed just six pounds at birth and had gained only four ounces during the week, but she was healthy and suckling from Elizabeth's breast without a problem.

Elizabeth had little energy, but she was well enough to walk every day in the hospital and knew she would regain her strength soon with Edward's help. One of the Italians in his gang had a daughter named Maria and he had arranged to employ her for a few weeks to help Elizabeth.

A week after Elizabeth had been home, she noticed that little Winifred's skin had turned yellow. As the baby was so small, Elizabeth was anxious for Edward to come home and take her to the hospital.

When Edward looked down at Winifred and saw her jaundiced face, he smiled and said, "Don't fuss. I have seen jaundiced babies in Wales and they have come good. Never mind, Bess, no cow is ever much good with its first calf."

His comment did not help Elizabeth's concern at all. She tersely replied, "Edward, we must go into Mackay! I canna stand it if our little wee bairn is sick."

Driving back from Mackay soon after, Edward smiled at Elizabeth. "I was right Bess - it was breast milk jaundice and the little one will be fine in a couple of weeks. You won't have any trouble with our next one."

Elizabeth thought to herself, 'That will be quite a long time in the future after what I've been through. A man canna ken what it is like to suffer so much birth pain. Who would want to go through that again?'

.o0o.

CHAPTER 23: Memories Of Wales

The cane-cutting season had started over four months ago in July. Each night the sky was lit up with cane fires burning all around the district. The fires were spectacular, burning fiercely, flames leaping up to twenty-five feet in the air, spreading ash and smoke, and sometimes black rain down on Elizabeth's home. Even the clothes hanging under the house were often stained with ash.

Elizabeth would often spot large cane rats scurrying across the bare ground near the house escaping the cane fires and dreaded the thought of one eventually finding its way inside the home.

Edward was always tired at night. He would rise before five, Elizabeth would prepare his food for the day, and he would then ride out on his bike to the cane field to meet his gang.

They worked together in a team - stooping low to chop the cane, straightening it, then topping the cane to remove the trash, and then piling it in rows. They would stop briefly to quench their thirst, with salty, black sweat dripping into their eyes, their clothing and their skin covered in ash from the burnt cane. After lunch the men would then load the cut lengths into the cane trucks pulled along by tractor truck, and the steam locomotive would haul the cane cages along the narrow two foot gauge rail lines to the mills.

It seemed to Edward that lifting and loading the heavy bunches of the burnt cane was harder than cutting it. The gang was paid by the amount of cane cut and he had to work as hard as the rest of the gang. They were all mates and they all relied on each other to keep up. Edward knew that the gang would soon get rid of any slacker in the team, as they needed to depend on each other to keep up in the section of cane they were cutting. They would then burn another lot of cane ready for harvesting next morning. One of the workers in the gang would keep a tally sheet of the cane they had cut each day because the whole gang was paid according to the tonnage of cane cut.

However, the tough hard work was affecting Edward's health. His wife would hear him coughing in long bursts many nights during the long cutting season and she was worried how it would affect him in the future. Elizabeth was now determined that one day they would leave this life and settle back in Victoria, where she would have support from her family, especially now that her baby was born. She thought that she could probably restart her dressmaking business as Janet was working for the Cowells and Jeannie Cowell had commented to her sister how much she missed Elizabeth's sewing skills.

Elizabeth received a letter informing her that her sister Isobell, her husband Callum and their children, Betty who was now fourteen, and their son Sandy had arrived in Melbourne from Scotland and were now renting a home not far from her mother. She longed to see them again and it increased her desire to move back, but it would not be easy persuading Edward. He had shown no intention of ever leaving North Queensland. He was earning a good wage and hoped that he would eventually save enough to own a small cane farm and hire cane cutters himself.

Edward and Elizabeth had visited his brother and Meg early in November before Winifred was born. Meg's baby Richard was now three weeks old, and with his blue eyes, blonde hair and sturdy body weighing over ten pounds, he looked every inch a Morgan, with the Welsh appearance of the two brothers. Meg had proudly held him out for Elizabeth to hold.

"Aye Meg, he is a braw bonny lad and no wonder you both are so proud of the wee one," said Elizabeth.

Meg smiled as she took Richard back into her arms, and Elizabeth was aware of a new softness in Meg's manner toward her. She wondered to herself, 'Has the birth of her baby changed Meg's attitude? Perhaps now Meg realizes how important it is to have the support of close relatives, and she must realize how fond Llewellyn is of his brother. They have been through so much together in Wales and often share those memories which are so special to them.'

Elizabeth was surprised and pleased when Meg said, "Elizabeth, our son Richard will soon have a little cousin, and we must try to see more of each other. I want our little ones to grow up loving each other, as we are family and Llewellyn wants Edward to make his life here, farming near his brother."

Tactfully Elizabeth smiled and agreed, but her inner thoughts were quite different. She knew that she had much more influence on Edward than his brother ever would. One day she would persuade Edward to move to Melbourne where she would be with her family.

Llewellyn was so different to her Edward, who was kind, generous and loved Elizabeth deeply, and if necessary he would always consider her happiness above his own wishes. Although Llew loved Meg and his son Richard there was a hardness in his demeanour and in his eyes. He was driven with ambition to become a very wealthy cane grower. He had often expressed his wish to Edward, to one day return to Wales and show off his wealth and prosperity to Meg's parents. They had regarded Llewellyn as well below their status and class. They had not wanted Meg to marry Llewellyn - an unskilled labourer who had no assets of his own.

Edward had no desire to ever return to Wales. He lived his life for Elizabeth and the family he hoped would one day grow. He was prepared to sacrifice any plans he might hold for the sake of Elizabeth's happiness.

Llewellyn was overjoyed at the birth of his son. They named him Richard after his grandfather. The brothers had been brought up in grinding poverty in the tiny cottage that the grand parents rented. Their parents had died soon after each other, of tuberculosis when the boys were ten and twelve years old. The cottage they had lived in was over one hundred years old, built with local stone with walls that were two foot thick.

The ceiling in his parent's home was barely six feet high. The huge fireplace with a stone mantlepiece above it almost filled the length of one wall. There was a large iron rack within the hearth for curing the bacon. A ladder at the far end of the cottage gave access to a small platform below the roofline where the boys slept. It was freezing in winter with just a little warmth from the heat of the fire below seeping up and across into their sleeping space.

Their great grandparents had lived there working as tenant farmers for the Earl of Powis, who owned vast tracts of land around Welshpool, and the Earl's court treated their tenant farmers poorly. The farmers of that generation knew they would never have the chance to own their own land in the Valley as they scratched to survive paying rent to Powis Castle.

The land had been granted as far back as the 17th Century, and passed to the Clive family. The estates were run like a feudal society with the peasant farmers toiling away, paying rents and living in poverty.

Their parents had rented the small farm, and, after their deaths, the boys were forced to live with their Uncle David who owned his own large farm. He had married his Welsh bride Gwendolyn, who was an only daughter of a prosperous farmer, and the land had passed to his wife on her parents' death.

After the Great War the farming land was sold to those tenants who could afford to buy the farms they had worked on for generations. The Clive family was deep in debt and forced to sell the farm lands, but they continued to live in Powis Castle. Edward's uncle was fortunate to own his farm because of his in-laws' prosperity.

David and Gwendolyn had two daughters who were spoilt and indulged by both parents. They were boarding at a private school in Cheshire and when they returned back home, they had no interest in mixing with their poor cousins who were only provided with farm work trousers, boots and shirts. Llewellyn and Edward did not have any decent clothing provided by the aunt and uncle who did not wish the boys to be seen around the village with their spoilt daughters.

Llewellyn would never forget the harsh impoverished life they had, working long hours on that farm, coping with the freezing cold of the winters, out in the fields and earning just one pound a week when they were in their late teens. With the birth of his son, and the prospect of buying up more cane land in the future, Llewellyn was determined to succeed and become very wealthy.

He often said to Meg, "I'll visit Wales when I have proved to those relatives of yours and mine that I am a man of means. I hope to give my grandparents and my parents marble gravestones in that small cemetery they are buried in, and we will arrive in the latest model large car. We're so lucky to have moved here away from that small village. I would never have had the chance to own a farm there."

.o0o.

CHAPTER 24: The Italian Connection

Maria stayed with Elizabeth for a month after she arrived home from hospital, helping with all the housework. Elizabeth enjoyed having another female in the house and the Italian girl was a wonder, helping the new mother cope with Winifred who slept for about two to four hours and would wake crying with colic. Maria was the oldest of four children and was not fazed at all caring for a new baby.

It was six weeks since Elizabeth had come home from the hospital with Winifred, before Edward spoke to his wife about restarting their lovemaking. Elizabeth would lie in bed with Edward's arm over her chest, and she could feel his erection pressing into her. He knew that Elizabeth was nervous and tired, with the baby waking so often during the night with her distressed crying, then Elizabeth rising to comfort her - he was not going to attempt to have sex without Elizabeth's permission. Elizabeth, however, was aware that sex was important for both of them, to feel that closeness and belonging to each other again.

Maria had now gone back to her home and Winifred was finally was sleeping for several hours at night. Edward kissed Elizabeth softly as he turned her towards him in their bed. He was surprised and thrilled when she responded so passionately.

Elizabeth shyly said, "I love you, but I canna bear the thought of having another bairn for a couple of years. Winifred is all I can cope with for quite a while."

Smiling in response, Edward lifted his pillow and produced a small packet and showed it to her, explaining, "I saw the chemist when we were in Mackay and he said that they have now made latex condoms which are cheap to buy, easy to use and you won't need to worry about becoming pregnant."

It took a long time for Edward to arouse Elizabeth sexually that night. She was relieved when he finally slid himself into her and she felt no pain. Her face was flushed with desire and she felt a wonderful uncontrolled throbbing deep within, rising to surrender her mind and body to climax with Edward. Afterwards they lay beside each other exhausted, but knowing that their love for each other made them complete. Elizabeth knew she wanted Edward as much as he had longed for her. From tonight she would equally share in their desire to meet their need for each other. Edward slept soundly that night knowing he had his Elizabeth back, and his patience was rewarded.

She was well worth the wait. He loved his Bess deeply. For her to be happy, and for him to share in that joy, seemed a far better future for him than anything else he might ever have considered.

Maria's mother Teresa Rosetti lived about four miles away on a small fifty-acre cane farm and they were their closest neighbours. Her husband Tony had purchased it in 1915 for three hundred pounds. Part of the farm was covered in dense tropical scrub that Tony had to clear, burning the logs and trash, and then planting his first cane crop between the stumps.

He worked long hours paying two cane workers to help, using a mattock for holing, then planting in the cane in rows, constantly weeding, and hoeing. They dug about 2500 holes for each acre cleared.

Teresa worried about Tony's health in those early years. He would come home in the evenings and collapse with tiredness, his back aching, sometimes falling asleep before he took off his blackened work trousers and shirt to shower.

Each year he cleared a new section of scrub, dug out and burnt the logs and stumps, and replanted new cane stalks. Edward had worked on Tony's land cutting cane in the twenties. They had used horses for drawing the cane trucks to the side of the permanent two-foot gauge rail lines. The trucks would join up to form a 'rake' of long lines. They were then picked up by the mill locomotive and hauled to the mill for weighing and crushing.

During the time Edward worked at cutting cane with his gang the cane farmers needed help in controlling the grub pest that was the larvae of the large cane beetle. Tony was desperate for help as he found his cane stools were dying. These 'stools' were the buds of new growth rising up from the stubble left after the harvest of the previous crop, and were an important part of a farm's continuing success.

The cane grubs were feeding on the roots of the stools and the cane would fall over or just perish. Edward and his gang managed to earn extra money by digging out the grubs and collecting the beetles. It was exhausting work but they were paid a high price by the pound weight of grubs and beetles collected. The cane farmers paid levies to the local Pest Board.

However the work was backbreaking and Edward said to his gang that he would never try to earn extra money digging out cane grubs again.

It was in an attempt to combat these pests that the American cane toad was introduced to Queensland cane farms in June 1935. Unfortunately the poisonous toads had little impact on the beetles, but spread rapidly across the State in subsequent years, doing terrible damage to many local species.

Tony told Edward when he arrived back in Mackay with Elizabeth that during the twenties, there were fifteen tons of beetles and grubs captured and destroyed and it made a big difference to the health of the cane crops now.

Tony's farm was now good level cane growing country with rich, dark, chocolate coloured soil and he was making a good living from it. He had built a Queenslander style home for his family and Teresa was very proud of her husband, who now could afford to employ others to do much of the hard work on the farm.

Tony Rosetti had also cut cane in the early nineteen twenties with some of the Italian gang whom Edward now worked with. He welcomed his daughter Maria earning some money, and helping Edward and his young family. Edward had given him a lot of help with his cane farm when he arrived in Mackay, clearing land and planting the cane. He knew how hard life was for the men during the cutting season which lasted nearly six months, and he was grateful that he was fortunate enough to manage to buy his own property and hire cutters to work for him.

Elizabeth had met Maria's mother, Teresa before Winifred was born. Teresa had taken Elizabeth into Mackay shopping several times and they had become firm friends. Teresa was thirty-seven, with long dark hair drawn in a thick plait hanging below her shoulders. She had a full busty figure, brown olive skin, brown eyes, and a full rounded face with a warm smile that lit up her eyes. She had four children and was well aware of how tough life was for a cane farmer's wife.

Teresa felt for Elizabeth, who had never lived in the tropics, as she tried to cope with her first pregnancy, suffering with the humid hot climate, beetles, snakes, and other insects, vermin and tropical downpours. Teresa knew how hard it would be for the young Scottish woman, rising early in the mornings to keep up with all the house work and washing that a cane farmer's wife had to deal with every day.

Elizabeth loved Teresa's warm generous nature. She would make fresh pasta, bring bananas and vegetables from the garden for Elizabeth and sometimes then share afternoon tea together.

In return Elizabeth had sewn Teresa two light wrap-around cotton dresses. They had chosen the cotton fabric together and Teresa was thrilled with them. They were a delightful contrast to the brown and black dresses she had been wearing. Elizabeth knew that it was her kind wonderful friend and neighbour that made such a difference to her life, which she still found hard to adjust to.

Meg had never been to visit Elizabeth in her home, which was about fifteen miles from their farm. It did disappoint Edward's wife that her sister-in-law was not bothered to make the effort. However Elizabeth and Edward visited them once a month. Meg was friendly, but still reserved towards her brother-in-law's wife. She never invited Elizabeth to join her to meet her friends in Mackay.

Meg's attitude reinforced how fortunate Elizabeth felt to have met Teresa, and they were now good friends. Her life was now so occupied with Winifred, managing the house, cooking and sewing, that she was not at all concerned about Meg's coldness towards her.

The last time that they were there, Richard was nearly a year old. He was pushing himself up to reach the table, and just about to walk. He was a strong, healthy handsome blonde haired boy with a happy nature. He enjoyed seeing his small dainty cousin Winifred, who was such a contrast to him in size. She would crawl across to Richard and hug him around the legs, forcing him to drop to the floor and then kiss him on his cheeks.

Llewellyn enjoyed seeing the cousins together, but he never failed to comment to Edward about how small Winifred was compared to his big strapping boy.

It delighted Elizabeth to hear Edward reply, "Llew, we have the most beautiful baby daughter a man could wish for, and I have my beautiful Bess. I am sure that we will have more children in the future and I don't care if they are girls, especially if they are like little Winifred."

.o0o.

CHAPTER 25: The Depression

Winifred was now almost eight months old and she had grown a shock of black curly hair. Her skin was as pale as milk, with rosebud lips, and her eyes were hazel. She was small and weighed just sixteen pounds.

Edward adored her, and whenever he approached she would raise her arms to be lifted in his hands high above his head. Winifred would gurgle and chuckle as Edward then cradled her in his arms and rocked her gently. He could hardly wait to shower and change into clean clothes to see his little daughter each evening, and put his arms around his Bess. Edward would say to Elizabeth that he now lived only for his family and repeated that he would do all he could for their happiness.

It was August and the cane cutting season had been going for a month. Elizabeth was into a routine like the other cane wives, preparing food, washing Winifred's soiled nappies and Edward's blackened, sweaty work clothes daily. She would then clean and sew her little daughter's cotton overalls and dresses, a job that gave her much pleasure.

Word of her sewing skills had spread via Teresa, and she now sewed for five of the cane farmers' wives. She did enjoy their visits, listening to the local gossip, sharing afternoon tea with them. These farmer's wives chatted openly about their lives, sharing in the similar problems Elizabeth faced, and missing their families too, scattered throughout Australia. She certainly was much more at ease with their company, than the occasional visit to see her sister in-law Meg and Llewellyn.

Queensland was now suffering the effects of the Depression and it was obvious when Elizabeth and Edward were in Mackay. They noticed a number of shops were now closed, and there were many houses in the town now sitting vacant.

Unemployment was now well over twenty per cent and climbing. Many men were on 'susso' – a 'sustenance payment', with work allocated by the Government according to a man's circumstances. The local council was employing many men with relief work: maintaining parks and roads, planting trees, working around the harbour and foreshores building sea walls, and doing reforestation works. A married man with a large family was given about five pounds a week and a single man about eleven shillings a day - it was barely enough to provide food. Anything else, such as supplementary food vouchers, shoes, and clothing was given out by church charities.

They saw several houses vacant close to Mackay because of evictions of families who could no longer meet their mortgage payments. One of the men of Edward's gang had purchased a home in Mackay, but he and his family were now living in a camp at the Mackay show grounds. The bank manager had shown no sympathy, even though their home was now vacant.

The cane industry was protected because imported sugar was not allowed, and the price in Australia was about three times the price overseas. The Government made sure that cane farming would be profitable, but the ordinary Australians and manufacturers paid high prices for sugar to make up for the subsidy given by the Government. This helped the cane cutters who were assured of work because the farmers could afford to pay them well compared to the normal pay.

Edward had heard many stories of suffering families and he had said to Elizabeth that when a swagman came towards his home, she was to be generous and make sure they had food for him. Elizabeth baked bread most days of the week as well as biscuits and cake. She always gave them a sandwich or a light meal. Usually they asked if they could help with some work, chopping wood, weeding, or washing the ash and dirt from the walls around the house.

Many of the 'swaggies' travelled long distances because the local councils only provided rations or work for a day and they were forced to travel from town to town. Edward talked to Elizabeth about how the 'swaggies' would 'jump the rattler'. He explained that they illegally rode on the goods trains throughout Queensland as the distances between towns were so great, and they were desperate to find work.

Sometimes a 'swaggie' would offer a couple of wild rabbits to Elizabeth for a shilling each. He would skin them for her and she discovered how delicious they were when stewed. Edward thought they were a treat as he had often eaten rabbit in Wales.

Teresa and Tony always had plenty of bananas or mangos in season to share and would drop off a few boxes of fruit at the showgrounds for the families forced to camp there.

Elizabeth wrote to her mother and sisters about every two weeks, always trying to sound positive about her life on the cane farm, even though there were many times when she dearly wished she were back in Melbourne nearer to her family. She knew Edward was better off here, as the Depression had been even more severe on working families in Melbourne.

Her mother Anne wrote often, and kept her informed about her family. Her sister Isobell had managed to find a job in a woollen mill near Richmond because of her skill as a weaver in Scotland. Her husband Callum, though, like many men was not able to find any steady work. He was doing relief work for the local council, working about four days a week and earning two pounds a week.

Their son Sandy was twenty and was working at the local abattoir as an unskilled labourer. He spent his days removing the manure, cleaning the blood-stained floors, and picking up and loading the raw hides of the animals. These were covered in maggots, which would fall down onto his cap and shoulders. The hides were slimy and putrid and after being loading onto the trucks, they were taken to the local tanneries in Preston to be turned into leather.

Anne said that Sandy did bring fresh meat from the abattoir, which was a huge help in keeping his mother out of debt. It was a rare treat to eat a leg of lamb that Sandy sometimes managed to acquire.

Her mother told her of her neighbour, whose family had been evicted from their home and had their furniture put out in the street. She had heard that about half the children at the local school in Collingwood had fathers who were unemployed. The men who had no savings and were destitute received a sustenance payment that was a pittance, and an extra two shillings for each child in their family. They were also given an ID card for groceries, milk, bread, baby food, firewood and some rent assistance.

The church where Elizabeth had married had set up a relief committee and the committee had found a rental for the evicted family who had been

Anne's neighbours. The house was unsewered and without a laundry, having just a concrete trough and copper outside the back door of the home.

Some of the families in the neighbourhood had moved to small towns in the country, because they could plant vegetables and potatoes, keep hens or a couple of goats, and catch plenty of rabbits.

The local butcher and grocer in Richmond had 'cash only please' signs on their windows. Not being able to buy 'on account' or credit made difficult for families to survive the week before they could get relief money for food. The workers who were on the dole were only allowed to buy sausages, forequarter mutton chops, and mince steak.

Her mother mentioned that she was spending some of her time helping to unpick woollen jumpers for the church, so they could be knitted up again as socks, children's jumpers or scarves. She was also given dresses to unpick, so that the unfaded fabric was on the outside. The women's sewing group then resewed them, or cut the fabric to make childrens' overalls or dresses. Once a week Anne helped in the church kitchen to make soup and hand out clothing, and the queues were always long, stretching more than fifty yards down the street.

Anne mentioned in her letters that it was just as well they were in Queensland, as Edward would find it very difficult to get any work other than relief work perhaps with a local Council working in the parks, planting trees or labouring on road maintenance, and even then that work was very temporary. Robert had told his mother that most of the building industry had shut down, and the Government in Victoria had mostly stopped Public Works building as it was impossible for the government to borrow, or get loans from overseas.

Robert was still working at the brewery, and Janet and Fay still had their jobs. Robert kept six hens in the back yard and grew some of their vegetables. Anne knew of one family who kept a cow in their small back yard and their children would pick grass every day for her. Their neighbour next door had cut a gate into their yard and helped feed the cow also. The cow kept both families in milk and butter. They would lead her out to the riverbank to supplement her feed each evening. Anne commented that she was lucky to have three of the family still working in such awful times.

Janet still worked for the Cowell family and she often spoke to her mother of the contrast between the lives of the people around Toorak and some parts of South Yarra, where the families were not affected by the Depression at all. Jeannie did not see Janet's mother very often, but she always asked about her friend. She often gave Janet clothing she collected from her friends as Janet had told her of her mother's work with the church ladies. Those dresses had been made up into some superb children's clothes for the destitute families in Burnley and Richmond, and some of them were altered to fit her sister Fay.

The big Melbourne stores were open, and Fay who worked in the city, had often remarked about the well dressed women walking along Collins or Burke Street with their hands clutching many shopping bags. The shops in the wealthy suburbs were also well stocked and the local women were still buying expensive clothing and shoes. There was plenty of credit available in the food shops around South Yarra and Toorak. Janet wondered whether these wealthy families had even heard of the Depression and the terrible effects it had on the some of the families where she lived.

.o0o.

CHAPTER 26: Rats

Some of the cane growers in the district surrounding Mackay did not want to burn their cane before cutting as it attracted lower prices than cut green cane. The Capes family who owned the cane farm where Edward worked decided to leave a section of cane green and not burn it, in spite of the protests of the Italian cane cutters. Burning the cane helped to get rid of the cane rats which spread disease, and which were now in great numbers as the wet season had started.

It was the last week in October and Edward's gang had been cutting the green cane for a week. The men were angry as the cane rats were in plague proportions in this area and they knew that they had a high chance of catching a disease from the pests. It wasn't necessary to touch or be touched by the animals to get sick. Contact with the soil that was contaminated with rat urine could cause a horrible bacterial infection.

Some of the men had seen other cane cutters who had become infected. Tony had mentioned that one of his Italian cutters who worked with him in the twenties had died after becoming infected. The men had decided to stop cutting the green cane and protest to their Union, which was quite powerful, to try to force the owners to burn the green cane before cutting it. Some of the cane farmers agreed to burn but many would not, because they got higher prices for it at the mill.

Edward came home after cutting the green cane for three days. He had a red rash on his arms, his eyes were very itchy, and he had a sore throat. He was not too concerned as he just thought he was getting a summer cold. The next night he had a temperature. He had vomited up his lunch and now was suffering with diarrhoea. Elizabeth saw that Edward's eyes were yellowing and she felt his forehead.

"Edward you are sick and ye canna go to work in the fields. Tomorrow we'll go to Mackay to see the doctor," she told him.

"Don't worry my Bess, I'll be fine tomorrow and the men need me on the gang. We have to keep our quota up for the mill," he replied as cheerfully as he could muster.

The next morning, however, Edward had muscle pains that seemed to spread across his body and his temperature was still high. Elizabeth panicked as she could not drive, and Edward was so sick. They had a long telephone line that also connected them to the Rosetti's home. She rang her friend Teresa who came over to the house within the hour.

She drove Edward, Elizabeth and little Winifred to the hospital in Mackay. After Edward was admitted Elizabeth waited with her friend for two hours. She was shocked when the doctor informed her that Edward had contracted a serious bacterial infection called 'Well's Disease' from the cane fields – a disease that was caused by cane rats.

The doctor explained, "Edward is to be isolated in a ward at the hospital as he is now jaundiced and he could suffer from liver or kidney failure. It is a very serious infection and we will have to hope Edward is strong enough to survive it. We can stop the vomiting and reduce his temperature but it is up to Edward to fight the infection."

Teresa put her arm around Elizabeth and said, "Edward needs to be here for a rest and to recover, Elizabeth. I will come over and help you."

Elizabeth was overwhelmed with the thought of her Edward now being so ill. How would she manage without him? She was so isolated from her own family who would have surrounded her with their love and support.

"Thank you Teresa. I dinna ken how I would have managed without your kindness and help," she said.

Edward had saved over three hundred pounds over the past year, and Elizabeth knew that she would manage for some weeks. She was also now sewing simple cotton dresses for some of the cane farmers' wives. Teresa had spoken to them of Elizabeth's skill at dressmaking and it was much cheaper to have Elizabeth sew for them than to buy dresses in Mackay.

Edward spent two weeks in the hospital and he was lucky to avoid serious permanent liver damage. However, he had no energy, and knew that he would miss at least a month before he could return to cane cutting with his gang.

His cane gang was shocked to hear of Edward's illness and they decided to go on strike, demanding that all the cane on the property be burnt before harvesting in future. It was now impossible to find other cane gangs to work on the Capes' property because the cutting season was in full swing, and word had spread about the possibility of contracting 'Well's Disease' cutting green cane. After two days of strike action by the cane cutters, the Capes family relented, and allowed all the cane to be burnt before harvesting.

It was mid-November before Edward was strong enough to head out to the cane fields again. His Italian gang was pleased to see their mate back again as he was such a hard worker. Even after his illness some of the men had to work hard to keep up with Edward as he was so strong. They knew he often did more than his share, loading the cane onto the trucks as well.

Elizabeth worried that Edward would not be strong enough, after over a month off work. The weather was now humid and hot, with frequent tropical downpours at night, sometimes causing the burnt cane to topple in the soft ground. It made cane cutting even more difficult, but at least Edward could manage a day or so away from the fields till the cane dried.

By now Elizabeth had come to intensely dislike living on a cane farm. She had been frightened by Edward's illness, and worried that he could once again catch Well's Disease, or possibly even die from another infection. The huge black cane beetles were crawling around under the house, sometimes flying into the bedroom and she was terrified at the thought of one landing on her body. Edward had caught two large pythons near the toilet and there were other venomous snakes living in the cane fields, feeding on the rats that still thrived there.

She was quietly determined to go back to Melbourne, but she did not wish to force Edward, as he still had plans to buy a cane farm. He spoke about his plans to his brother when he saw him, and Elizabeth knew that within two years they would probably have enough money to put down a deposit on a small farm of about eighty acres.

The cutting season finished at the end of December and it gave Edward and Elizabeth a chance to relax from the grind of the long cutting season. The Italians had left the property and headed back to Mackay, or further north to catch up with their relatives who owned cane farms.

One of the Italian cutters, Alberto, who Edward worked with, said that about half the farms in the Herbert River district were now owned by Italians. His Uncle Georgio had arrived in 1906 and had had the chance to get work as a cane cutter. The federal Government had decided to deport most of the Pacific Islanders who had been working on the large sugar plantations as indentured labourers in that year.

It was not the fault of the Islanders themselves – many had been brought in by unscrupulous plantation owners to work as little better than slaves. The big sugar plantations were broken up into small holdings and sold fairly cheaply, because the owners no longer had the benefit of cheap Islander labour to cut the cane.

Alberto's uncle worked long and hard and bought his own small farm, as did other Italian and European migrants. Georgio sent money back to Italy and brought out a woman called Gina, who he had known in his village. It was an arranged marriage and they now had three children. Alberto enjoyed helping his uncle on the cane farm and meeting his cousins each year.

When the United States applied immigration quotas in the 1920's, the Southern Italians came in large numbers to Queensland. Many of their relatives in Ingham had written to people in the villages in Southern Italy telling of their new prosperity as cane farmers, encouraging them to migrate to Australia. Georgio also hoped to buy a farm near his relatives around the Ingham area as it was almost a 'little Italy' there with so many Italians making it their home.

Georgio told Edward how some of the white locals resented the Italians and their success as cane farmers. White local groups often protested, causing even more anti-Italian sentiment around the district. They said that although there were plenty of good local people who supported the Italians, they were often abused by others as 'white dagoes'.

Edward had heard some of the men in the hotel talking about the invasion of the 'Olive Skins' taking their jobs. He knew though that most of the white men he listened to would not last too long cutting and loading cane. It was a job that only strong, resilient and tough men could do.

.o0o.

CHAPTER 27: A Day At The Beach Has Consequences

Edward was fully recovered, and enjoyed spending more time with Winifred who was three months past turning one. They had more time to visit Llew and Meg, and Richard loved playing with his little cousin. Richard was a sturdy, mischievous boy, and Elizabeth kept a close watch on their play together as he could now stretch up and open the screen door to the garden. The last time they had visited, a spider had bitten Winifred and a large lump had appeared on her thigh.

Once again Elizabeth wished they could move south where she thought she would not have to confront frogs, spiders, snakes and beetles as well as suffer the high humidity which made her so uncomfortable for months of the year.

In May Edward decided take Elizabeth and Winifred to Eimeo Beach, which was about twenty minutes' drive from Mackay. Elizabeth had not visited a beach since she arrived at Mackay, and was looking forward to sharing a day away from the farm. They drove under a canopy of mango trees near the beach with coconut palms lining a section of the sheltered bay. It was a perfect day with just a whisper of breeze and a sapphire blue sky overhead. Edward carried Winifred to the water's edge and she squealed with delight as her toes dug into the soft sand.

After a swim Edward's muscled olive skin glistened as he strode out of the water, and Elizabeth thought to herself, 'What a wonderful body my Edward has. Not a mark on that smooth skin.' Later they picnicked under the shade of the trees. Edward put his arms around Bess and kissed her softly.

Before they headed back to the farm Edward took them to the large hotel overlooking the beach. They sat out on the deck with Winifred sleeping in Elizabeth's arms. Edward headed to the bar and bought back two icy cold beers, each with about half an inch of froth on the top.

Elizabeth had not tasted beer before. She had memories of her father in Scotland coming home after drinking - the shouting and violence that then occurred was embedded forever in her memory. The poverty they had suffered because of her father's drinking, and the fear the family endured whenever he drunkenly entered their 'but and ben' gave Elizabeth a hatred of alcohol. She had seen so many families suffer from it.

Hesitantly Elizabeth took just a small sip of the beer and was surprised that it was so cold and, yes, it was refreshing after their long day at the beach. Edward smiled as she handed him back half of the glass of beer, saying, "Och it tasted fine Edward, but I would never get a taste for it. I dinna want you to get too much of a taste for it either."

The sun was setting across the bay, reflecting onto the water and drenching the sky in colours of gold, deep pinks and soft purple. As they headed back to the farm Elizabeth thought, 'Aye, if we could have many days to share like this one, then maybe I could get used to our life here, in spite of the heat and humidity.'

Later that night after Winifred was settled into her cot and was sleeping soundly, Edward lifted Elizabeth into his arms and walked into their bedroom. They were passionate in their lovemaking, taking their time to arouse each other, till it was Elizabeth who clasped Edward tightly to her, with her legs wrapped around him. As Edward thrust into her, they climaxed together, and then collapsed with their arms around each other, feeling deeply satisfied, physically and emotionally, in their love for one another.

It was July when Elizabeth realized that she had missed a period and was feeling nauseous in the mornings. She remembered that after their day at the beach in May Edward had not used a condom. She was certain that she was about two and half months pregnant. Elizabeth realized that her idea about moving back to Victoria was now impossible. Edward was her husband and she needed his love, and also his support financially if they were to prosper and raise two children.

She told Edward as soon as he had showered. His blue eyes lit up with the news and he clasped Elizabeth into his chest and kissed her.

"What a wonderful present you've given me! Winifred will now have a brother or sister. We can ask Maria to come and help you. I've always wanted a family and now we'll have two children to share our lives."

The cane cutting season had began and Edward was again working with his Italian gang. They were staying in the 'barracks' and cooking meals for themselves. Edward told them his news the next day. They insisted he come back with them that evening to the barracks and share some wine with them. Afterwards he staggered back to his house smiling with happiness, but when he tried to hug Elizabeth, she slapped him hard on the face. She had never seen Edward drunk, and it shocked her.

She pushed him away and burst into tears.

"Och, Edward, I canna stand drunk men. Keep away from me. I never want to see you like this again. If I do, then I will leave you."

Winifred was now a year and half and she was standing beside her mother. She looked up at her father with her thumb in her mouth. Edward tried to lift her up into his arms but Elizabeth grabbed her from him.

"No drunk man is going to hold ma baby!"

Edward attempted to explain what had happened, but to no avail. With unhappy memories of her father swirling in her head Elizabeth strode into her bedroom with Winifred and shut the door.

He did not sleep with her that night and he was miserable. To be beside his Bess in bed, feeling her body tucked into his with his arms across her breasts gave him such contentment, and even one night without her beside him caused him sadness at his stupidity. He lay awake thinking of what had happened and, harmless as one evening's celebration had seemed at the time, he vowed that it would be the last time he would ever come home drunk. He loved his wife deeply and he could not imagine life without her or little Winifred. Now he was to be a father again he would not risk life without his Bess and his family.

Elizabeth was relieved that her morning sickness did not last more than three months. Now that Winifred was walking, sitting in her high chair to eat, playing happily with her toys and having long sleeps in the afternoons, she was managing to cope with all of her daily chores. She had time to have a rest and sew in the afternoons.

Her baby was due sometime in January in the middle of the wet season, when the humidity and heat were at their peak. However the cane cutting would be finished and that would be a huge relief. Not having to wash every day would make things easier, and Edward would be there to help her and take care of Winifred. Elizabeth longed to see her family, but she remembered how exhausting the journey was from Melbourne, and now the prospect of traveling that journey with two little children was almost too daunting to contemplate.

Edward made sure there was plenty of wood cut, stacked up near the stove as well as beside the copper. Since that time he had come back after drinking with his cane gang, he had never had a drink with them, and did all he could to help her at the weekend. He had told his gang about Elizabeth's anger. They laughed good-naturedly, but agreed that they would not tempt him again, at least whilst Elizabeth was pregnant.

Elizabeth felt her first contractions on January the fifteenth. The gripping pains were coming every hour and Elizabeth lay on the bed with Winifred at her side. She put her little hand on Elizabeth's stomach as another sharp contraction caused it to upheave.

Winifred was two, and she was excited to soon have a new brother or sister. She constantly asked questions, and Elizabeth explained that the baby was in her tummy and was almost ready to be born.

Winifred asked, "Will it come out of your belly button?"

Just then Edward came into the bedroom and lifted Winifred high into the air. He swung her around, and as she laughed with joy, she forgot about her last question. Elizabeth knew that with her second baby now on the way, she needed to get to the hospital as soon as possible. At least this time she knew what was to happen, probably within the next twelve hours.

After a hurried but careful drive, Edward left Elizabeth at the hospital, and drove back home with Winifred. The midwife had said that the baby would not be born for at least another twelve hours.

Trevor was born early in the morning. Although Elizabeth was in labour for ten hours the birth was easier, but still it was an overwhelming relief to have that last contraction, and to hear the midwife say that she was now fully dilated.

"One last push Elizabeth, and you will have your healthy baby beside you," she was told.

Elizabeth leaned up on her elbows as she felt another contraction, and pushed till she thought she would be torn apart.

"It's a beautiful black haired healthy boy," came a voice from somewhere past her legs.

Trevor was wrapped in a soft towel and placed beside Elizabeth. She looked down at her son and held his tiny hand, and wished Edward had been there to share this moment with her. Instantly her love for this tiny baby flowed deep within her and she had a sense of wonder as she looked and saw how perfect he was.

Edward arrived about four hours later. He walked into the ward and saw Elizabeth with their son in her arms.

He strode across the room as Elizabeth smiled and said, "We have a wee black haired son, Edward."

Edward leaned down and kissed his Bess. He had tears in his eyes, and he could not express the joy, love and relief he had looking at his beautiful son and knowing that Bess was well. He had stayed awake most of the night worrying about his wife, hoping that she would not have to go through as much pain as last time, when Winifred was born.

Now he saw them both safe and well, and he was more than content.

.o0o.

CHAPTER 28: Elizabeth Goes South

Trevor was two months old when Elizabeth suggested to Edward that she wished to visit her family. After his first two weeks at home, Trevor had slept for over six hours at night. It gave Elizabeth the chance to recover quickly from his birth. Maria had worked five days a week helping with the housework and entertaining Winifred in the afternoons whilst Elizabeth rested. This help had given her the chance to feel fully fit again, but Maria had now left to look after her mother as she was recovering from pneumonia.

Anne was thrilled at the news of a new grandson and once again Elizabeth hungered to see her family in Melbourne. Elizabeth was concerned about discussing a possible trip to Melbourne with Edward, but her longing to see her family again, and introduce her mother to her grandchildren, overwhelmed any thought of not approaching Edward and attempting to convince him that this was the ideal time to make the trip.

Edward was very unhappy at the thought of his family leaving him for over three months, especially the idea of Elizabeth taking such a long journey without him, but Elizabeth was persistent and very persuasive, especially after they had sex.

Elizabeth lay in Edward's arms and pleaded with him to allow her to take the long journey to be with her family again.

"Ah canna take it much more Edward," she pleaded, tears filling her eyes. "I've twa bairns to care for noo, and I canna be worrying about snakes all the time. Now she's walking I dinna ken where Winifred is half the time.

And what with the new bairn to worry aboot, I'm half out of my mind. Mother has nae seen ma bairns and ah just feel homesick for my family all the time."

Edward could not bear to see his Bess so unhappy and he agreed to let her have her way.

"I'll miss you so much Bess. Now that we are close to owning our own farm next year, I've got to stay here and make a go of it. It is our future."

Edward's blue eyes looked so forlorn that Elizabeth felt pangs of guilt. She loved him dearly and knew that she would ache for him while they were apart, but the longing to be with her mother and sisters was overwhelming.

"I'll be back in three months," replied Elizabeth. "I promise."

He knew that she missed her family and longed to see her mother and her sisters, especially with the two children. He also knew that Elizabeth had never fully adjusted to life as a cane farmer's wife and hoped that maybe this journey would help her to realize that their life was here with each other, working to own their own place and giving their children a good life as well. If he stopped her from going, his Bess would possibly resent him and he could not bear the thought of losing her love. What right did he have anyway, to stop her from seeing her family? He reluctantly agreed with Elizabeth, but he was deeply unhappy at the thought of losing his family for three months.

Trevor was now three months old. They had gone to Mackay the previous week and purchased the ticket to Melbourne.

The evening before Elizabeth was to leave for Melbourne she said to Edward, "You'll never know what it means to me. Many times I've felt so miserable here but I would never leave you, and go without your consent. You have given me that freedom to go. I dinna think many other husbands would allow their wives to go away on a long journey without them."

Her husband's huge body seemed to sag and he came forward and hugged Elizabeth tightly. His blue eyes filled with tears and he quietly said, "If it is what my Bess wants so dearly then I'll not stand in your way."

Elizabeth looked up at Edward and so many thoughts crowded into her mind. 'This caring wonderful man who loves me so much and who I feel so safe and secure with, who has never shown any ill temper or been ruffled by my outbursts of anger, and now is reduced to tears by a ticket.' She reached out and held his hands as a strong emotion of love for him surged within her.

Edward smiled and he swirled Elizabeth into his arms with barely an effort and carried her into their bedroom. They both shared a desperate urgency to give themselves completely to each other. Time seemed to balance like a huge ball on a needlepoint, threatening to topple at any moment.

Gently he placed her on their bed that had withstood the passion of their lovemaking over the past years. As their bodies fused into one, Elizabeth felt an elation, a passion culminating in a climax that seemed be more intense than she had ever experienced before. Edward knew that he could never love any one else with such a desire and completeness as felt for his precious Bess.

As they lay in each other's arms, Edward could not imagine that this would be the last night he would ever spend with Elizabeth in Queensland. If he had known what the future would hold for them, he would never have let her leave the next day.

That next day was hot and stifling. It was mid April, Elizabeth's cotton dress clung to her back, her face was flushed, and her hair clung to the back of her neck, wet with perspiration. It had not rained for two weeks as it was now the end of the wet season, but it was still humid. She looked out of the car window and the hot air seemed to have sucked the life out of even the shrubs and trees.

As Edward drove along the dusty road away from the farm, Elizabeth gazed across at the young cane about two feet high, now a rich succulent green contrasting with some of the land that had just been cleared of bush, with the stumps still showing above the ground.

Elizabeth was anxious, and her stomach seemed to be churning inside her as Edward approached the train station in Mackay. Winifred stood on the back seat and put her arms around Edward's neck, and Elizabeth held Trevor in her arms. He was just over three months old and she was still breast-feeding him. Trevor was such a placid, healthy boy and slept soundly for hours at night. He looked up at Elizabeth, smiled and gurgled. She thought that it was the best time to make the long journey while he was still being breastfed. She would not need to bother with clean bottles for his milk and he would sleep for much of the trip.

Edward adored his children, and although he had agreed to Elizabeth's request to go to Melbourne, he knew he would miss his family every day. Already he silently regretted giving in to his wife, as he was actually very concerned as to how she would manage the trip with their two children, but he was not prepared to upset her, after he had agreed to Bess's request. They had lived on the farm for almost four years and in his heart he realized that it was unfair to stop Elizabeth from seeing her family. After all, he had his brother and sister-in-law living only a short distance away and he loved sharing the 'old times' they had together in Wales, and appreciating Llewellyn's knowledge of cane farming that he shared with him.

He could not leave the farm because in two months they would be cutting the cane again. He could not afford to be without a job in Melbourne. The Depression had hit Melbourne with a much greater force than in Mackay. The letters Elizabeth had from her mother told such a sad story of poverty and unemployment around the working class suburbs in inner Melbourne in 1934 and now 1935.

"A man has got to be able to work, Bess," he said. "If he isn't able to work and support those he loves then something dies within him."

At the end of this season, Edward planned to put a deposit on a small farm. He knew it would secure the future for his family. His brother had recently bought another eighty acres of land that was partially cleared, and the price being paid for the sugar cane was enough for a man to make a good living providing he owned his own farm.

It would no doubt have helped Edward if his brother had repaid the money that had been loaned to buy that first farm, but there always seemed to be some reason why that couldn't happen. The birth of a child, or a new land purchase or deal that tied up funds. More than once Elizabeth thought that her husband was simply too soft-hearted to push the point with Llew, and privately wondered if her brother-in-law would ever settle the debt. In fact, he never did.

Edward walked into the train station carrying two suitcases, one under his arm, and holding Winifred's hand, whilst Elizabeth carried Trevor. He had booked Second Class sleeping berths for them on the new train called the 'Sunshine Express' that had only just come into service. It had left Cairns on the long fifty-two hour journey to Brisbane, stopping at the large towns along the coastal route.

The Queensland Government was keen to promote tourism and had upgraded the train service with new carriages. Elizabeth and Edward were very impressed with the carriages, which had leather seating and electric lighting as well as electric fans. The interiors were fitted out with varnished Queensland timber panelling. Edward was relieved to see that Elizabeth's sleeper berth was comfortable and even included a washbasin in the cabin. They could not believe the contrast with the train in which they had travelled to Mackay four years ago. The steam train journey would take about thirty-five hours to Brisbane, and Elizabeth planned to stay there overnight before catching the train to Sydney.

Edward carried the suitcases into the sleeper berth and he lifted Trevor into his arms.

"Well my little man, you will be a big strong boy before I see you again."

Winifred was too excited about her long train journey to understand that it would be quite a while before she would see her father again. "Why can't you come with us, Daddy?"

Edward could not answer her. He kissed her and felt as if his heart would break. He kissed Elizabeth deeply and waved goodbye to the children as he left the cabin. When would he see his family again? Would they be safe on the journey? How would he manage without his Bess and the children who he lived for?

The rhythmic sound of the train wheels was enough to send Trevor into a deep sleep after suckling on Elizabeth's breasts. It was a relief to know that feeding Trevor on the long journey would not be a problem providing she kept hydrated for the whole trip.

As they travelled Winifred ate sandwiches and Elizabeth read one of her favourite books to her, *'The Little Engine that Could'*. She also loved her book of fairy tales, especially the tale of *'Little Red Riding Hood'*, and Elizabeth had made sure she had packed it too.

There were light refreshments on board in the buffet carriage, which meant Elizabeth did not have to worry about leaving the train. However Elizabeth sprang awake during the night when she heard a loud rattle of the handle outside her door. For a moment her heart raced as the rattling continued. Elizabeth had locked the door and placed her suitcases there. She heard a slurred voice shout out, "Let me in, woman!"

Then the porter arrived and there was a scuffle in the corridor as he gripped the man's arm and said, "Get along with you. This is not your carriage!"

Before the train chugged into Brisbane Central Station early in the morning, Elizabeth fed Trevor and packed her suitcase, putting Trevor's wet nappies into an overnight bag she had put into her suitcase. The porter knocked on the door and apologized for the disturbance during the night. He was very sympathetic toward this attractive woman. He had observed her walking along the corridor with a baby and a little girl and he noticed that there was no sign of a husband to help. He carried Elizabeth's bags to the large cafe at the station and then arranged a taxi for her. Elizabeth was relieved to leave the train as her back ached and her legs were stiff, but she had managed to get some rest when the children were asleep.

Edward had arranged for Elizabeth to stay at the *Peoples Palace* in Brisbane. It was a temperance hotel that provided inexpensive "working class" accommodation for travellers, and was almost across the road from Central Station. The Salvation Army owned it, and no alcohol, gambling, or "other evils" were allowed on the premises. Edward had stayed there in the '20s and he knew it would be safe and comfortable for his family.

After the long train journey it was a relief to stay in a hotel room with good facilities. The staff members were very helpful and provided a cot for Trevor in her room. Elizabeth was longing to wash the soiled nappies, bathe the children and herself.

The next morning Elizabeth and the children caught a taxi and made their way to South Brisbane Station, as it was the terminus for the standard gauge line from Brisbane to Sydney. It then went on to Albury, where she would have to change trains again.

Elizabeth wondered, 'What were the State Governments thinking about when the three Eastern States all decided to have different gauges for their train tracks?' It was a decision that all would regret in the future, as it would be an enormous expense for those Governments to change to a standard gauge between capital cities.

The sleeper berth on the train to Albury was not as modern as the new

Sunshine Express, nor as clean. However once again the porters were understanding and kind and they brought drinks and sandwiches to her cabin and provided extra blankets. They had seen her struggle with Trevor along the corridor. He was restless and crying loudly through lack of sleep on this part of journey as his bunk was firm and uncomfortable.

Elizabeth briefly left the train at Sydney Station where most of the passengers disembarked. The sleeper berth was cleaned and sheets changed when she returned, which brightened her mood. She was beginning to wonder whether her determination to leave Mackay, which meant that Edward would not see his family for months, was selfish and cruel on her part.

She looked down at Trevor's face and his dark innocent eyes looked up into her face as he smiled at her. Elizabeth picked him up, and she promised herself to love and cherish the children so carefully, till Trevor and Winifred could be reunited with their father. She was beginning to realize how much she would miss Edward, and how unselfish and caring he was. He had given her the chance to see her family, even though it had hurt him deeply.

That last night they had made love, full of passion for each other as the thought of parting from each other was uppermost in both Edward and Elizabeth's minds. It was now a precious memory, and the realization of their long parting saddened her profoundly. Had she done the right thing leaving Edward, just to see her mother, sisters and brother again? However Elizabeth had never adjusted to the life of a cane farmer's wife in that climate, and her heart ached with a longing to see her family again, and to have the chance for her mother to see her grandchildren.

Albury was the terminus for the main Southern line to Melbourne. The porter helped Elizabeth with her suitcases, as they walked along the long platform to the ladies' waiting room to freshen up herself and the children, and then into the large refreshment room. Elizabeth was amazed at the huge ornate Italianate station building with all its facilities available for tired travellers like herself.

What a relief, though, to climb aboard the train for the final leg of the trip. The locomotive steamed out of the station. This last leg of the journey was to take about eight hours.

This time Elizabeth did not have a sleeper berth, but luckily she shared the cabin with another woman who was in her mid thirties. That meant company and conversation – welcome after travelling with the small children.

It was half an hour before Elizabeth would meet her mother at Spencer Street Station and she began to sort through the clutter that spread along the seat of the train. She threw everything into her large overnight bag. Phyllis, the lady who shared the carriage, had entertained Winifred and read her fairy tales. Trevor had been fed at Albury and he had slept soundly for most of the journey.

At last, Melbourne, and her beloved family.

.oOo.

CHAPTER 29: Three Months And More In Melbourne

It was now more than three months since Elizabeth had stepped from the train to be lovingly welcomed by her mother, Anne and her sister Janet.

How proud she had been to hand Trevor across into her mother's arms, saying, "Trevor is your third grandson, and a fine wee lassie and laddie I have brought to Melbourne to see their grandmother."

Janet had lifted Winifred into her arms and said, "What a bonnie lass we have here! I am your Aunty Janet."

Living in the small cottage in Burnley and talking every day to her family, Elizabeth's Scottish brogue had become almost as broad as when she had stepped off the ship so long ago. Janet and Fay were thrilled to have their sister back with them, especially now they could help with their little niece Winifred and nephew Trevor when they came home in the evenings.

Elizabeth longed for Edward's letters. He sent her money every fortnight and proudly told her that he was in the process of buying a small cane farm near his brother, and the following year they would be settled on their own property.

His letters to Elizabeth always closed with, 'I miss you Bess, come back soon. All my love, Edward.' But over three months had passed, and both the children had been sick. Winifred had suffered from bronchitis and Trevor was teething, as well as suffering from a chest infection.

Even Elizabeth was now missing the warmth of the Queensland winters in Mackay and wondering whether the children would have been much healthier there. She also had not been feeling well herself, so she had written to Edward and delayed her return for another month, but now it was her husband she was homesick for. Elizabeth's heart ached to be back with him, but she was struggling to breastfeed Trevor and she was feeling so poorly each morning herself that it would be impossible to contemplate taking the long train journey back just yet.

There were mornings when, as Elizabeth rose to pick up Trevor, she again felt like vomiting. Trevor was still being breast-fed, but this nausea had been with her for the past two weeks. She was constantly tired managing such an active, strong baby as well as Winifred, and decided it was time for Trevor to be fed from a bottle. He was now over six months old.

Elizabeth thought that maybe she would feel much better soon, and would be able to book her fare back to Queensland. Edward longed to have his family back with him, and it was selfish of her to delay the journey any longer.

She ran her hand down her thickening waist and stared at herself in the mirror. 'Och, I've put on weight here. It must be mother's rich Scottish cooking.'

Elizabeth grabbed her corset that lay across the chair and fitted it around her stomach. She pulled the strings of the corset tightly around her body and buckled the belt in front. It took more effort each passing day to keep her body in the shape it had been when she first arrived in Burnley.

Her mother noticed the increasing roundness of Elizabeth's belly and asked, "Are you sure you're not pregnant?"

"How can I be? When I left Edward, Trevor was three months old and I was still breast feeding him. I thought ye couldnae get pregnant whilst breast feeding a baby."

Anne looked again at Elizabeth's rounded stomach. 'Perhaps Elizabeth is just putting on weight. My figure is nothing to write home about,' she mused. 'I'm now thirteen stone, and Elizabeth is probably just taking after her mother.'

Trevor was six months old and Elizabeth had stopped breast feeding him. He was now very strong and was pulling himself up on his cot. Soon he would be crawling.

Whilst Elizabeth was in Queensland her older sister Isobell had come out from Scotland with her husband Callum, her twelve-year-old daughter Betty and her two boys.

This morning Elizabeth wanted to talk with Isobell and persuade her to get rid of four dogs that her son Sandy had dragged into his home for his mother to feed. There were also five stray cats that lived under the house.

Isobell's husband Callum had not been able to find work as the Depression was biting hard for working class people in Melbourne. He had started earning two pounds per week from the local Council planting trees, weeding and collecting rubbish around the local Burnley Park but often was now drinking it away at the local hotel.

Callum had been a coal miner in Dunfermline and he had been a proud miner with some status.   He had enjoyed the comradeship of the other miners and shared in some of the tragedies that often happened with the dreadful mine accidents, including his father-in-law's death in a coal mine. The coal mines had gradually closed near Dunfermline and he had been persuaded to migrate by Isobell.

He had no other skill as he had started work in the pit at fourteen. Callum found it demoralizing not to have regular work and he could see no end to the poverty around him. He was ashamed that he could not support his family as he had managed to do in Scotland, and sought some solace at the hotel.

Sandy had regular work at the abattoirs nearby. If not for his small wages, the free meat he managed to scrounge from the abattoir and the help from Hugh, his older brother who had found work driving a small goods truck Isobell would have starved, or relied on the local church meals and small amounts of money from her mother.

Elizabeth loved Isobell deeply. Isobell was her oldest sister and was thirty-eight. She had wonderful large, gentle blue eyes that always seemed to twinkle and sparkle when she spoke, and she possessed a rich humour that drew people around her. Her soft nature would never say 'no' to stray animals, and her son brought scrap meat back from the abattoir to feed them. With the tiny back yard that they had, it was impossible to keep it from smelling or to avoid stepping on dog faeces. The walk to the toilet was becoming a frightening experience as the bounding, cheerful dogs leapt up to be greeted, almost knocking Elizabeth over whenever she visited them.

It was true that with the meagre amount of wages coming in, they still could hardly afford to feed the family let alone several stray dogs, but this was Isobell and she was not prepared to see them starve, or on the street again. Isobell had faced many problems in her life, but nothing had taken away the deep kindness she showed to everyone around her. No matter how serious or sad a problem, Isobell always found a way to give people a small glimmer of hope, and provide plenty of humour as well.

Elizabeth headed down the road towards the other end of Burnley Street close to the river and opposite the abattoirs, where Isobell and Callum had rented their small cottage. The smell emanating from the abattoirs opposite Isobell's house was overwhelming and brought a sickening nausea up into her throat.

Close by was the local tip which stretched down to the Yarra River's edge. It was a poor area to bring up a family but the rental was cheap and Isobell and Callum felt lucky to even manage to get this place. At least it was only half a mile from her mother Anne, who loved having her family close to her.

Elizabeth walked down the narrow lane at the back of the house. It was used also by the night cart man as the small back flap of the toilets opened onto the lane. Elizabeth hated the tiny back yards of the inner suburban tenements. That was something good about her Queenslander, with space all around her and fresh air to breathe. She could easily forget about the ash from the cane fires, the snakes and large insects that so terrified her when confronted with the stench of the tip and the abattoir here.

Elizabeth opened the wooden gate that led onto the lane and heard Isobell's voice saying, "Och there's our Bessie, she'll no put up with these dogs. I canna think what she will do with them."

The dogs were lying at the entrance to the back door. It was almost eleven o'clock and the sun was beating down, making the dogs drowsy with the warmth on their backs.

Two families who lived nearby had left two of the dogs. One family had been evicted for unpaid rent and had moved to inland Victoria. Isobell and Callum had been friendly with them, and it saddened her greatly to see their meagre belongings covered with a tarpaulin out on the street.

The Depression had hit poor families hard. The sustenance payment or "susso" was only a small amount of money for unemployed families - not even sufficient to provide enough food, even with help from charities. It was impossible for many families to keep up the rent payments, even on the 'slum' houses. Isobell had seen many people evicted over the past three years, and there seemed no end to the poverty and suffering of people living near her in Burnley and Richmond.

While it was hard for them, Isobell's family were in a slightly better position than many others. Sandy at least had a job, and Callum worked two days a week for the local council in the parks. Isobell had work weaving in a factory in Richmond, drawing on skills learnt in Scotland working in the linen factory in Dunfermline. When Sandy brought meat home, it kept the dogs fed, as well as providing many meals for her family and often helping out their neighbouring family with fresh meat or bones for soup.

The father, Reginald, was a friend of Callum. He was an unemployed 'Digger' from the Great War, and the Returned Sailors and Soldiers Imperial League of Australia (the RSSILA, which in later years became the RSL) had granted him ten pounds to help with the family's fares to move inland to a small town near Ballarat. They also offered to pay half of his wages for six months, and the local Council who were willing to provide relief work, would pay the other half. The local relief committee was to help find a rental for them. Of course Isobell offered to take the family's border collie called Dusty, hoping that eventually they would take him back once they had resettled.

Another neighbouring family had left during the night to avoid the unpaid rent, and Isobell's son Sandy found their small fox terrier wandering in the street. The boy brought it into his home. He loved animals and it was he who found the other two dogs scavenging in the local tip, which was close to his home. He promised his mother Isobell that he would find homes for them, but they had been in the yard for a month.

Both 'tip dogs' were mongrels. One was a labrador retriever and the other one was part boxer. Decently fed on meat scraps from the abattoir where Sandy worked, the dogs were placid and friendly.

Isobell's back yard was tiny and the four dogs were always gathered around the back door, often barking and leaping up for affection each time anyone appeared outside. On one visit, Elizabeth had almost fallen as the part boxer leapt up with his front paws reaching just under her breasts.

She'd staggered back against the back door, shouting, "Gang away with you!" It was then she vowed that she would get rid of them to help Isobell.

The prop clothesline had fallen over several times as the dogs chased each other around the tiny yard. Sandy was constantly being told to pick up the dog mess, but he came home from the abattoir so late most nights that it was often just left for someone to tread in as they crossed the yard to the outside toilet. Elizabeth could not understand why her sister Isobell was so soft and allowed the dogs to be brought into the yard at all.

Elizabeth reached down to tie pieces of rope around the necks of the two mongrels who stood up for her. They wagged their tails in such a friendly greeting that Elizabeth felt momentarily guilty about what she was about to do to them.

The back door opened and Isobell trotted out, saying, "Elizabeth, leave them alone. They are not eating much and Sandy is getting plenty of scraps from the abattoir."

"No, I said that I would help you and I will. That Callum of yours is as weak as you are when it comes to it. You said yourself, you canna have them all in the yard much longer."

The older sister sighed and said, "Have a cup of tea before you go. I ken you are determined to take these dogs. Ye are a determined lassie, and I wish I were as practical as you. I dinna care if my Sandy brings a few dogs into the yard to feed, but they are a handful at times."

The fox terrier and the border collie seemed to know what might be ahead of them, and they bolted out through the back gate into the lane for some short-lived freedom.

As the nausea again swept up into her throat, Elizabeth decided that at least she'd be satisfied to take two, and leave the others. She also suspected that Isobell would not allow the other two to be removed as her family had become especially fond of the terrier and the collie.

Isobell did hope that the collie would one day be reunited with his family. Reginald's two children loved Dusty, and had only been persuaded to leave him when Isobell promised to look after him till he could be reunited back with them.

The effort of dragging two reluctant large dogs up to the dog pound at the local Council yard was almost more than Elizabeth could cope with. She headed up along Burnley Street dragging her two unwilling mongrels behind her. Suddenly the labrador jerked his head sharply sideways and freed himself from Elizabeth's grasp. In the effort to grab back the piece of rope that was attached to the fleeing dog, Elizabeth let go of the other piece of rope. The boxer mongrel grabbed his chance of freedom and bolted back up the road with the rope trailing behind him.

Elizabeth could have sat down on the gutter's edge and wept her heart out. She felt so miserable, depressed and useless. She missed having Edward to confide in, to help her with the children, and she ached with such a longing at night, to have his arms around her again and to make love to her. The effort of dragging the dogs made Elizabeth feel sick and, as she turned to go back to her sister, she leaned over the gutter, retched and vomited up the sour bile rising into her throat.

She dragged herself back to her sister Isobell and was greeted by the four dogs now in the back yard again. They did not seem to bear any grudge at their experience and greeted her enthusiastically, which caused Elizabeth to burst into tears.

Isobell came out and laughed at the sight of the dogs, but then saw Elizabeth's tearful face. She hugged her sister closely and said, "Noo, we'll have that cup of tea."

Elizabeth tearfully said to Isobell, "I must go and see a doctor and find out why I feel this way. I just canna go on like this any longer. I need to get back to Edward but I feel too sick to take that long journey."

Isobell had thought for a while how pale Elizabeth had been. Her mother had commented to her a few times saying, "How wan our Elizabeth looks lately."

Anne made the appointment with her doctor the next day. When she looked at Elizabeth after her ordeal with the dogs, she realized that something was not right. Elizabeth did not eat her supper and could barely cope with feeding Trevor. Something would have to be done.

.oOo.

CHAPTER 30: Unexpected News, Twice Over

The stiff boned corsets that Elizabeth had been pulling tighter as her stomach had swelled, and that were the fashion at the time, came off in the doctor's surgery.

Elizabeth climbed onto the examination table with trepidation. The doctor gently probed her abdomen and asked Elizabeth, "When did you last have a period?"

"Ah never had a period since ma son was born and I've just stopped breast breeding recently."

"Well I've some news for you. I'd say you were over five months pregnant. Surely you knew, Mrs Morgan? You must have suspected that you were pregnant."

Tears sprang into Elizabeth's eyes. She remembered that last night when she parted from Edward and they had been so passionate and intense in their lovemaking. 'That was ma going away present,' she thought.

The doctor's words echoed through Elizabeth's mind. "Are you sure, Doctor?" She knew what his answer would be before he spoke again.

"I'm positive. A doctor isn't likely to make a mistake about a question like that when his patient is over five months pregnant."

He tried to reassure Elizabeth, saying, "Cheer up now. It is not the end of the world. I know your man is in Queensland and you need his love and support at this time, but I know your mother will stand by you, as will the rest of your family."

"But Doctor, it will probably be another six months before Edward can come back here. You know how the situation is here. Work for men like my Edward who is a cane cutter would be impossible to find. I feel that all I can cope with now is ma baby son Trevor, and a two year old. How can I manage with another new baby? It will be very difficult to get back to Queensland with a new wee bairn, a one year old and Winifred."

"Don't worry Mrs Morgan, you'll find that if you give yourself plenty of rest, you'll handle it well. Don't forget you've a wonderful mother to look after you."

Elizabeth abandoned her corsets from that moment and released her swelling belly. Why hadn't she kenned before this? The old wives' tale of not getting pregnant whilst breast feeding had been blown away. Elizabeth felt foolish to have ever believed in such a myth. As Elizabeth sat on the train on the way back to Burnley, her mind was in a whirl. She found it difficult to comprehend the fact of this new life stirring inside her now, but the memory of the last night with Edward and their passionate love-making was clear and that, without doubt, was the start of this new life now growing inside her womb.

'How stupid and ignorant can one be?' she thought. 'Of course these symptoms I've felt in the past months have been identical to the ones I felt when Trevor was conceived. The nausea in the mornings, the vomiting. How could I have ignored such obvious symptoms? At least there is no doubt as to the date of conception of this baby. Och, I gave Edward a gift greater than even he had bargained for.'

Elizabeth was certain that Edward would welcome their new baby with the same joy that he had greeted their other two children. He had always said that he wanted a large family, but because economic conditions forced them to be practical, they had settled on a family of two till they were settled on their own cane farm.

Anne put her arms around her daughter and said, "It's not the worst thing that can happen to a lassie. Be thankful that you have your health and a man to stand beside you, even though such a distance separates you. The time will pass quickly and once you and Edward have settled into your own place, you'll be glad you had this baby now instead of waiting and planning. You're thirty-two now, and if you give Edward a family quickly, you'll be able to cope with their growing up whilst you are still a healthy young lassie."

It was now impossible for Elizabeth to think of travelling north and Edward was in the middle of the cane cutting season. He needed to remain there, as they now needed to save more than ever.

The next four months passed rapidly in spite of Elizabeth constantly thinking of Edward. Elizabeth's health had improved and her mother made sure that she rested each afternoon and insisted that she did not avoid eating meals. She busied herself sewing for the new baby, as well as Trevor, Winifred, and her sisters Janet and Fay. Isobell managed to get woollen fabric offcuts from the factory and Anne's neighbour allowed her to use her sewing machine.

Edward now knew about her pregnancy, and after the initial shock of the discovery, he was thrilled to have his young family expand to three. He was worried for Elizabeth, but knew she would have plenty of help and care in Melbourne with her family around her. He opposed any suggestion of Elizabeth travelling back to Mackay.

He had been sharing meals with the pickers in the 'barracks' and Marie had come over twice a week to help with the washing and cleaning. The cutting season was exhausting for the men, but the pay was about three times that earned by unskilled workers in the town. Edward was still planning to buy a small farm after Christmas, and now that he would have three children to care for he had even more incentive to save. He still held the hope of help from his brother, or at least the repayment of the old debt.

Elizabeth's body had stretched into a full roundness, and she felt that the birth would be within the next week or so. Trevor was one year old now, crawling up the narrow passage into the small kitchen every day to be greeting by his Granny. Elizabeth was so grateful to be surrounded by her family and have them take over so much of the care of Trevor and Winifred. At least not realizing she was pregnant for almost five months, the time had gone much more quickly than when she had carried Trevor and had suffered so much morning sickness.

With each passing day Elizabeth was looking forward to the birth with more and more enthusiasm. Her stomach looked huge, the veins on her belly were blue, a varicose vein had appeared on her right leg, and it was now a struggle to reach down and pick up Trevor. She hoped it would be a girl but the sex was not so important as long as the baby was healthy.

Elizabeth had felt many strong movements stirring inside her during this last month, but the doctor had reassured her that all was well and the baby was lying inside her, perfectly naturally, and its heart beat was strong and sound. It was now almost nine months since she had left Edward. How often in that time Elizabeth had thought of the night of the new baby's conception. They had been so passionate, triggered by the thought that it would be months before they met again. Never had Elizabeth imagined that it would be this long.

'Och – What's that wet stickiness I feel between my legs…?'

Elizabeth walked calmly down the passage into her bedroom knowing that the baby was almost due to be born. It was only a small red stain but it was the start of a sequence of events that she knew, and gave her the urgency to get to the hospital in Melbourne.

It was the Queen Victoria Memorial Hospital in Lonsdale Street that Elizabeth wished to go to, as it was managed by women, and staffed by women. "For Women by Women, for the benefit of poor women uncomfortable with male doctors," she had read, and Anne's doctor recommended it. Elizabeth tried to remember exactly what had happened before the birth of Trevor and the vivid memory of his birth came flooding back to her.

"Mother," Elizabeth called, "I think it's time we went to the hospital. I think you will have another grandchild some time tonight."

Elizabeth's suitcase was already packed with the new baby's needs as well as two new Swiss cotton nightdresses Elizabeth had sewed herself. Anne carried Elizabeth's case and they slowly walked up the short distance to the tram stop at the top of Burnley Street.

The tram trundled along towards the city and Elizabeth started to feel her first contraction but it was a mild one, lasting only a few seconds. She was frightened though, and clutched Anne's hand tightly.

"Dinna worry, Elizabeth. It is just a short trip to the hospital at the top of Swanston Street, and that bairn will no come just yet," her mother reassured her.

What a relief it was to walk into the Hospital and be welcomed by one of the midwives, just as a sharper contraction seized her body, causing her to hold her breath and grit her teeth. Elizabeth was taken straight to the ward and a hospital gown replaced her clothing.

Another contraction surged through her, making her grimace in pain. She silently said to herself, "I must relax, breathe in and out slowly, and not tighten myself."

The midwife gently raised Elizabeth's legs and examined her internally. "You are now three quarters dilated and it will not be too long before your baby is born. Try not to push until I tell you, my dear. You are doing well."

The contractions were now coming every two minutes and it was difficult for Elizabeth to concentrate on her breathing. She did have such a desire to push, as she just wanted this excruciating pain to end, but the small dark-haired midwife's reassuring voice said, "Wait, it is not long now. I can just see the crown of your baby's head."

Another powerful contraction caused Elizabeth to cry out, and then she heard the midwife say, "Bear down now, dear, the baby's head is almost through."

It was an intense relief as the firm brown hands of the midwife eased the shoulders out and the pain was finally over. Elizabeth was relieved that the feeling of terror and agony that she had felt with the birth of Trevor was not there with this baby. Her whole being relaxed as she saw the midwife lift the tiny baby up by her feet and she heard the soft cry of her new child.

"It's a girl, Elizabeth. You must remain calm whilst I get the doctor to check you out," explained the midwife. "You did not give her a chance to make it into the labour ward to help you. However I knew you would be brave enough to face the birth and we are well trained to help you."

As the midwife hurried out of the labour ward Elizabeth was left alone, with the baby having been wrapped in a soft cotton blanket and placed in a small wire cot. She had a feeling that something was wrong. She knew that the after-birth had come away freely because Elizabeth had seen its vivid red mound in the kidney dish. Yet her body still felt swollen and tight. She still felt the urge to push again, and was now in more pain.

The sister hurried back into the ward with four other young women medical students and a grey haired senior woman doctor. The students clustered around the bed and their faces peered into hers.

"Be calm, Mrs Morgan. We've something to tell you," said the gentle midwife who had delivered her baby.

Elizabeth looked up at the sister with a very anxious look. 'Surely there is nothing wrong with the little girl that had grown inside me, protected and nourished for nine months,' she thought.

Elizabeth was very pale. She closed her eyes for a moment and spoke in an anxious and worried tone as she opened her eyes and looked up into the doctor's face. "What is it? Tell me. Is anything wrong with my baby?"

How could there be anything wrong? She had heard her baby cry, seen her tiny face, and then she'd been placed into the small cot. They would not have left her baby alone if something was amiss with her.

"It's alright, Mrs Morgan. We've something very important to tell you." The grey haired woman doctor leaned over and spoke quietly to Elizabeth. "Now you have a beautiful little five and half pound daughter, but in about ten minutes you are going to give birth to another one."

Before these words from the doctor could fully register in Elizabeth's head, she felt another sharp pain and had a huge desire to push and push out this other tiny being that was tucked inside her womb. She was shocked as the words of the doctor sank in.

"These students are here because this time it will be a breech birth. That means that your baby will be born bottom first, instead of head first as most other babies are born. They should all watch a breech birth if possible, as part of their studies, and very few babies are born this way."

Another sharp contraction caused Elizabeth to cry out. The birth canal was still stretched after the first birth and the doctor said, "Try not to push, as I will now try to grab the tiny feet of your twin, and pull your baby into the birth canal. This will help me to deliver your child naturally."

Gently and very carefully the doctor's hand found the pair of tiny feet inside Elizabeth's vagina and manoeuvred them past the baby's bottom. Elizabeth's next sharp contraction caused her to bear down and push. The doctor then managed to gently pull the shoulders through, and finally the baby's head, face up. At last another pair of tiny feet were being held up above Elizabeth.

"Another girl, you are a lucky woman." The doctor turned to the students and said, "You are fortunate to witness a breech birth, especially twins. This is probably why Mrs Morgan had no idea she was carrying twins, as one is lying on top of the other one in the womb and sometimes it is impossible to know."

This baby burst out crying filling her lungs for the first time with fresh air and Elizabeth knew that she was fine.

However just at this moment Elizabeth did not feel at all like a "lucky woman". How would she ever get four children safely back to Queensland when Trevor was a year old, and now two new babies to cope with? Elizabeth knew that the double birth would cause many problems for her and Edward.

Somehow as she let herself be washed and cleaned she gradually drifted into a deep sleep, her body totally relaxed but now drained of most of her energy. As she dozed off she realized that any problems that emerged would be surmounted with the help of her family and her dear wonderful Edward.

The following morning the twins were brought into the ward and both were put into Elizabeth's arms. She looked into their tiny faces. Both were less than six pounds in weight, and they stared up at her with open eyes. She held them close to her and felt a surge of love for these two helpless babies, as yet nameless.

One of the twins started coughing and her little face turned a bright red. Before long the other one was coughing as if in sympathy for her sister. The midwife came into the ward and looked down at the twins.

"The babies both look very stressed and I will have to take them back to the nursery to calm them down," she said.

A mild panic rose up into Elizabeth's mind as she saw them being carried away. 'Edward hasnae seen his twins and it will be a while before he does. Please let nothing happen to them. They are part of our precious family and I already love them so.'

That evening the grey haired senior doctor came into the ward looking very grave.

"Mrs Morgan, your twins have a chest infection and we are worried that it might get worse. We will have to keep them in hospital till they recover and it could take a few weeks. We will have to get you to express your milk so they can get all that goodness. You can see them but we will have to feed them, using your breast milk."

Elizabeth burst into tears. Edward had not had the chance to see his beautiful twin daughters. He did not know yet that the girls had even been born, and now they might lose these precious babies.

The doctor put her arms around Elizabeth. "My name is Doctor Grieg - Janet Greig, and I will be doing everything I can to save your babies."

The doctor gave a determined, reassuring smile. "After all, I was there for the delivery of one of your twins, and we are not going to lose them to an infection, after all that you, and especially your babies have been through to come into this world. Your husband will be most anxious to see his new children and we will make sure he does."

.o0o.

CHAPTER 31: Living With Isobell

When Edward received the telegram telling him of the arrival of his twin daughters, he was not told how dangerously ill they were. He laughed and shouted across the paddock to his cane cutting mates, "Bess has done me proud this time boys! I've two wonderful new daughters! Bess had twin girls in Melbourne two days ago."

The Italians gathered around Edward smiling and congratulating him, giving him powerful slaps on his back. "Two bambina piccolas for Elizabeth! You are lucky man!"

Edward longed to rush down to Melbourne to be beside Bess and his four children, but the cane cutting season was to last another three months and he knew he must finish this season before he could go south. They now would need his money more than ever. It was hard to get his head around the thought that he was now a father of four, but Edward was thrilled to have his family double in size. He had always wanted a large family, and to think that there were now twin girls was something he could never have imagined.

By now Edward had saved over three hundred pounds and this would be the foundation for the start of their new life together. Bess would be able to find a home where his children could grow safely. The dream of ever owning a cane farm was perhaps now too difficult to think about. He was needed in Melbourne with his Bess. However he knew with a deep conviction that the best decision he and Bess had made was to break away from the 'Old Country' and come to Australia where there were so many possibilities in the future.

Elizabeth stayed in the Queen Victoria hospital for a week, providing milk for the twins, but it was obvious that their health was deteriorating. They had lost some of their birth weight, they were listless, their cough was worsening and they both had a fever. Elizabeth was frightened for her babies, and, as she observed their rapid breathing she knew that they were becoming dangerously ill.

Doctor Janet Greig was keeping a close watch on the twins and she worried that they might have acquired the infection at birth, or during their delivery. Elizabeth did not want to let Edward know how seriously ill the twins were, as he would try to come back to Melbourne to support her and she knew that financially it was much better for him to stay at work. They would need all that he could earn in a season. However she decided to have the twins christened in the hospital just in case they did not survive.

Although Elizabeth considered herself an agnostic, she was not sure as to the depth of Edward's belief, so at least the twins would be given names and baptized as Christians. Doctor Greig arranged for a minister to come to the hospital, and Elizabeth and the doctor stood beside him as the first-born twin was named Isobell after Elizabeth's sister, and the other was christened Anne after her mother.

It was Doctor Greig who suggested to Elizabeth that a new drug had been discovered that could possibly treat the bacterial infection that the twins were struggling with. By now, they possibly had pneumonia, and were desperately ill. It was an antibiotic sulpha drug that had been discovered in the early thirties in Germany and was now available in Victoria. The doctor had read that it was 'the first medicine that could effectively treat a range of infections inside the body'.

Elizabeth was desperate to save her twins and readily agreed to the doctor's request to try the sulpha drug, called prontosil, which had been trialled successfully on many patients. She went back to Anne's home as her mother and her two sisters were caring for Winifred and Trevor; but she knew they were missing her, and Elizabeth was anxious to be with them again.

Every day for the next three weeks, Elizabeth travelled into the Queen Victoria hospital to be with the twins, and also to express her breast milk. Doctor Greig was convinced they would have an even better chance of survival with her breast milk as sustenance.

Gradually the twins started to improve. Was it a co-incidence that their improvement started after their baptism? Elizabeth had arranged for the baptisms for Edward's sake. He had spoken to her of his attendance at the Welsh Chapel when he was a young boy.

'Maybe this is what he would have wanted just in case the twins would not survive,' she had thought.

However, there was no doubt in her mind that it was the sulpha drugs administered in the hospital that actually did save their lives. Elizabeth would always remember the courageous doctor who was prepared to take the chance on the new drug, and had done the research into this new antibiotic that eventually would save thousands of lives in World War Two. Edward would now have the chance to meet two healthy babies when he arrived in Melbourne at the end of December.

Elizabeth decided to move in with her oldest sister, Isobell. Her home was close to her mother's. Isobell's daughter Betty was now twelve and already she was very helpful, taking Winifred for walks most afternoons. They did have a spare bedroom now that Isobell's oldest son Hugh had left home. Betty offered to help with the twins once they left the hospital and Elizabeth would sorely need it with four little children to cope with.

Callum raised no objections. He was not a strong-willed man, and usually deferred to his wife Isobell. Elizabeth was a more determined character than her sister, and when not at work Callum was often to be found at a nearby bar, retreating into a beer glass.

It was little Winifred, now just three, who could not settle into the new household. She would scream and scream and simply refused to quieten. Perhaps it was not hard to understand as she had missed her mother and now was in another house with strangers.

Elizabeth also spent much of the day feeding and caring for the tiny twin babies once they came home from the hospital. Winifred was not at all interested in the intrusion of these two babies into her mother's life. She started sucking her thumb and making sure she was heard.

Twelve-year-old Betty was given the task of caring for Winifred after school and it was soon tiring listening to her loud screams. Betty became impatient with Winifred's tantrums and eventually would tell the little girl tell to 'shut up'. When being taken out for a walk, Winifred would follow Betty, only removing her thumb from her mouth long enough to say, "Shurrup Betty."

Trevor was now one year old, and his Grandmother insisted that he now drink from a cup instead of his bottle, telling him, "Aye, there are twa bairns below you now, and it's time for you to grow up."

However he was a dark haired gentle, placid boy and was too young to worry about his new home. He had his mother back to snuggle up against.

The twins were just over a month old before Elizabeth was allowed to bring them into the home from the hospital. They had fully recovered, had gained weight, and Elizabeth was able to continue to breast feed them. She realized that she would never have managed but for her niece Betty and her girlfriend Elsie. They took them for a long walk each afternoon, and helped care for them.

The young girls loved taking the twins out. Often they were stopped, as the neighbours were curious to see the twins tucked into the large pram. Twins were not a common sight, and it caused plenty of gossip in Burnley as their father had never been sighted with Elizabeth.

.oOo.

CHAPTER 32: No More!

Elizabeth had received Edward's letter three weeks ago telling her of his intention to return to Melbourne in early January. It was now just one week till they would be together again. She constantly thought about his return and her desire to restart their sex life, which was such an important part of their relationship.

However, Elizabeth was constantly tired and wondered how she would cope with the physical demands of that sex life again. She was awake so often during the night managing the twins' needs, and often Trevor would wake when one of the twins cried and disturbed the other one. At present sleep was much more important to her than sex, but would Edward understand?

It was Edward, with his patience in their lovemaking, who had opened her mind and heart to the indescribable feeling of her body, and the joy of sex when she reached a climax with him. He had written so often of his deep desire to make love with her again. Yes, she did want him beside her again, and she would not deny him his need for her, but she was terrified at the possibility of becoming pregnant again.

Clearly it was now essential that she find some form of contraception that would be effective. It was unthinkable to have more children. The twins were just three months old and now weighed just over ten pounds. They were only just over five pounds in weight when they were born and had struggled to survive that first month. They took up so much of her time and she was grateful to her sister Isobell and her niece Betty who mainly took care of Winifred and Trevor.

She was breast-feeding the twins every three or four hours and had to supplement her milk as well, as they were now gaining just under half a pound in weight each week. Although they slept up to fourteen hours, Elizabeth was awake at least twice each night and was constantly tired. There were over a dozen cotton nappies needing to be washed and aired each day, as well as the rest of the soiled clothing. Having to light the outside copper, and soak the washing in the concrete troughs before using the hand wringer, meant that the laundering was a task that took her most of the morning.

'Aye,' Elizabeth thought, 'I canna bear to have another wee bairn. This house is already overcrowded. We need to find a place of our own soon after Edward arrives.'

Elizabeth decided to speak to her sister Isobell. They were sitting having a cup of tea after finishing the morning's laundry and she spoke about Edward's return.

"I am so worried about the thought of another bairn to cope with. What can I do to prevent it happening?"

Isobell smiled and replied, "Dinna worry lass. I've been using a sponge and I smear it with '*Lifebuoy*' carbolic soap. It'll kill any stray sperm. It has worked for me for years. Sometimes I get a rash but I dinna fuss about that."

Elizabeth did not comment, but she thought that this method would be unsatisfactory for her because she was not keen to insert phenol soap into such a sensitive part of her body each night.

Two days later Elizabeth walked along to her mother Anne's house late in the afternoon hoping to speak to her sister Janet, who had become engaged to Tom nine months ago when Elizabeth was living in her mother's home.

She had met Tom often when he visited, and was impressed with the way he reacted towards her children, showing a genuine love and care for them. He was smitten with Janet and constantly showed it with many small intimate gestures, touching her back lightly, placing his arms across her shoulders, sneaking in a kiss on her cheeks and muttering secret words into her ear whenever he thought they were alone.

He had easily gained the affection of Anne, as Tom never appeared without a box of chocolates or a small cake for her. It was no wonder Janet's mother welcomed his frequent visits as well.

Elizabeth had remarked to Janet, "Och, ye have a braw young man there, Janet and aye he'll make a fine husband and father for your children one day."

Janet and Tom often took Winifred out to the Burnley Park at the weekend, bribing her with ice cream. However, Tom genuinely enjoyed being with the children, lifting Trevor up into his arms when he arrived much to Trevor's delighted gurgles. In some way he provided the male support that was now missing in their lives with the long absence of Edward. By the time Edward would see Trevor again all memory of his real father would have been long lost from the little boy's mind.

It was obvious to all that Janet and Elizabeth were sisters. They were so similar in appearance, both having fine pale milky complexions with just a hint of pink blush on their rounded cheeks. They both had hazel eyes, dark eyebrows, black hair, soft full pink lips and small slightly turned up noses. Elizabeth was taller by two inches with slim hips and long slender legs, whereas Janet had inherited her mother's thicker hips and thighs.

Although Janet was four years younger than Elizabeth she seemed much more worldly. She had been living in Melbourne for four years, working, mixing with her friends, constantly meeting them in the evening at the latest huge dance hall, '*The Trocadero*' in the heart of Melbourne. That was where she had met Tom. It held well over 2000 people and was the most popular dance venue in Melbourne. Janet had mentioned it many times to Elizabeth, because she marvelled at the massive deep blue ceiling inside the hall, filled with twinkling stars, and the huge Dutch windmill outside, complete with rotating sails.

Janet now had an air of confidence that Elizabeth knew she lacked. She wanted her younger sister's advice. "Och Janet, I now have four bairns and I am terrified of having another wee'un. Edward just has to look at me and I am pregnant. I canna think what to do."

Janet laughed and took Elizabeth's hands in hers.

"Well aye, Tom and I are in love and he is eight years older than me. He uses the new latex condoms but we are still careful. We are getting married in July and I dinna want to be pregnant before then. I'll get Tom to buy some for you. Women simply won't ask a chemist for condoms, and some men would not go near a chemist if they know a woman is behind the counter to serve them. Many men just don't bother to do anything, but expect their wives or girlfriends to sort out something. No wonder we see so many large families around here living in such poverty with too many little mouths to feed! I am sure Edward doesn't want more bairns now either. You both have enough to manage as it is!"

Elizabeth could not disagree. She knew that Edward would use a condom willingly, but that there had been times when, swept up in the passion of a moment, neither of them had thought to use that precaution.

"Never again!" she said to herself firmly. "I'll no compromise our wonderful sex life, but we simply canna deal wi' yet another bairn. From now on, it will have tae be on!"

.oOo.

CHAPTER 33: Edward Returns To Melbourne

It was the end of January when Edward finally arrived back in Melbourne. At last on his way to see his beloved family, he walked along Burnley Street.

As Edward passed the abattoir he heard the loud mournful bellowing of the cattle. It was a hot day and the strong stench coming from it permeated the air, filling his nostrils, causing Edward to almost stop breathing for a moment to avoid the awful smell. His thoughts turned to his time in Wales, where he had looked after the cows and calves for his Uncle David.

The rolling green Welsh paddocks reached out to the hills in summer, and the cattle were so content and peaceful, chewing their cud and munching the fresh grass. He had loved leaning his head against the flanks of the cows as he milked them, taking in the sweet smell of fresh warm milk, and the scent of fresh clean straw he placed around the floor of the barn. Watching the birth of a calf as it struggled out from its mother, and the gentle licking of the cow to stimulate her tiny calf to rise to its feet, always filled him with emotion.

He took care of the poddy calves when they needed to be fed by hand. They would wrap their soft tongues around his fingers as they slurped up the warm milk. Edward thought to himself, 'I would love to own a couple of cows one day and be able to provide my family with all the milk, butter and cream they would need. Maybe one day Bess and I will find that place for us.'

As he turned the corner into Barkly Street, he told himself that whatever happened, he would never work in an abattoir to earn a living. It was a place of torture, with no thought taken about the animals' suffering. In this hot dry heat of January, the cattle were forced to stand out in the sun, packed together and possibly even lacking water as they waited to be slaughtered the next day.

He thought, 'What a contrast this place is compared to the wide spaces on the cane farm with the young green canes stretching out across to the horizon.' He had left it all behind just a week ago.

The weather in Mackay in January had been very humid and hot, draining his energy and causing his shirt to be soaked in sweat within half an hour of starting to work outside. He knew Elizabeth had hated the climate there in the summer months, especially the heavy tropical downpours that so frequently occurred, bringing out the insects, frogs and snakes she was so frightened of.

January in Melbourne may have lacked the Queensland humidity, but often suffered from hot dry north winds sending the air temperatures up over ninety degrees. Today was one of those days and the burning, dry heat, beating down onto his body, was likely to last for days, without the possibility of relief or a cool change. At least in North Queensland he could always rely on a heavy storm that would bring on lush green growth, freshening the air, filling the creeks and water tanks.

Edward wondered whether he could adjust to living here, as he had loved working out in the fields as part of a team with his cane gang. That desire to own his cane farm now seemed a distant dream that would never be achieved. His brother now was in the process of acquiring another cane farm and had been saddened at the thought of probably not seeing Edward again for years. Llew realised that Edward would always put Elizabeth's wishes ahead of his own, and he knew how much she had longed to be with her family in Melbourne.

The four hundred pounds that Edward had saved was now needed urgently to purchase a home for his family. His young Morgan clan had doubled in size whilst he was in Queensland. It was hard to get his head around it all, let alone wonder how his Bess had managed to cope with four children, especially twins now just three months old. She would need all his love and help, and his steady wage coming in each week if they were to get through the next few years.

Edward walked along Barkly Street, which was opposite the Yarra River, and at least he looked across to some bush growth - tall gum trees with tall dry yellow grass stretching to the banks of the river. It was a polluted waterway, the damage caused by some of the many industries operating further upstream, pouring their waste into it.

He approached what would be his new temporary home, living with his wife's sister and her family. The frontage of their dual tenement home was tiny, only about seventeen feet across with the front door on the narrow veranda about six feet from the fence. At least it was built of brick, but there were windows only on one side of the house with a very narrow laneway leading to the back yard. This was a working class area and most of the homes were similar. Others were made of rough weatherboards looking worse for wear, desperately needing a paint job.

Edward knew that Isobell and Callum rented it and the landlord was not interested in spending a penny on it. He probably knew that he could easily rent it to someone else if the tenant complained too much, without bothering to do any repairs.

The Welshman's face and arms were a deep golden brown, his hairline had receded, now highlighting his high forehead, and showing a prominent bald patch on the top of his head. He had deep blue eyes, showing wrinkle lines at the sides. His strong powerful six foot frame was still well muscled, highlighting his slim hips. Edward's hands were large and roughened, with the backs of them a deep dark brown, and his knuckles gnarled and wrinkled, showing all the signs of the tough physical work he had done over the past years.

As he stood at the door, knocked and then stepped back onto the veranda, Edward's stomach was churning with anxiety at the thought of seeing Elizabeth again. He was nervous and anxious about their reunion. A full year had passed and he ached to hold her in his arms again. The year apart from his Bess and the children had caused Edward much sadness. He thought of them constantly and it left a huge ache in his heart.

His distraction had been in coping with the hard physical work on the cane farm, having the company of his cane gang in the in the evenings, where he usually shared meals (and sometimes too much alcohol) with them, then falling into his bed exhausted after the long day in the fields. That routine had dulled his mind to the pain of Elizabeth's and his children's absence.

The thought that he had to save money if they were to have any future also kept him from heading to Melbourne sooner. The shock of discovering that his family had doubled in size provided all the incentive Edward needed to work hard, not that he was a man who had ever really required such prompting.

Edward rang the doorbell and he heard the sound of footsteps coming down the passage. The door opened and there stood his Bess.

Elizabeth had known that Edward would be arriving the first week in January, but she was unsure of the exact day. It was such a shock to see him standing there with a huge smile spreading across his face, his blue eyes staring down at her, shining with love.

For some moments Elizabeth was speechless. After being apart for so long, living with the memory of Edward and her longing to be with him again, now suddenly seeing him standing before her was difficult for her to take in.

"It's been a long time, lass, and I've missed you so much, every one of those days we've been apart."

Elizabeth shyly went towards Edward. He lifted his Bess up into his strong arms and kissed her passionately. It was now over a year since he had said "Goodbye" on Mackay Station. His eyes watered as he looked into his beloved wife's eyes. Elizabeth opened her lips to him, returning his kiss with equal passion. The time apart fell away and she knew nothing had changed in their love for each other.

"Bess, you have done me proud, and I swear that I'll not be parted from you again. I've longed to have you beside me with our children. Now we have four to care for, and that is a large enough family for any man to help bring up."

Edward looked down the dark passage and saw little Winifred running towards her mother. The girl flung her small arms around Elizabeth's leg and buried her face in the folds of her mother's soft cotton dress. She peeped up at the tall, bronzed stranger still holding her mother. Edward bent down and stretched out his arms to his beautiful little daughter. She had lost her chubby baby fat and was now over three years old.

Winifred turned towards him with wide-eyed fright and shouted, "Go away, go away!"

Her thumb then went into her mouth and she showed no sign of recognising this stranger. Winifred clung to her mother and Elizabeth lifted her into her arms and kissed her.

"Dinna ye be frightened. This is your father come back to us."

With her mother's reassuring arms holding her tightly, Winifred dared to turn her little face towards Edward. She looked into his deep blue eyes as he smiled and said, "I've come back to my little one."

Somehow lost fuzzy memories of being held up in the air by strong arms and hands, being tucked into a cot, feeling contented and loved by someone who was part of her past, calmed her. But Winifred was still determined to make sure her mother kept a tight hold of her.

Elizabeth led Edward into her bedroom where the twins were sound asleep in two cane bassinets. Just then Trevor lifted his head up from his pillow, reached up to the bars of his cot and pushed himself, to stand with his small hands clutching the rails. He was smiling at Elizabeth and was not at all concerned at the strange man staring at him.

Trevor was three months old when Edward last saw him, and now, he thought, his chubby dark curly haired son was probably walking. How he had missing seeing his son growing into such a handsome little boy.

Edward could hardly take in the sight before him, and he was surprised when Trevor reached out to be lifted up out of the cot by his father. The boy's chubby fingers traced around Edward's mouth as he stared into his father's eyes. With Trevor in his arms, Edward stepped across to the bassinets.

Carefully putting down his son, he reached down and gently placed his huge brown hands on the top of each twin's head. They were tucked securely in their soft blankets.

The babies were now three months old. Edward looked down at them just as one of the twins lifted her head and opened her eyes. He touched the soft blonde hair on her head. To Edward they looked so fragile and tiny, and he was overcome with emotion. He thought to himself that he would be frightened to hold such tiny infants. They each weighed just over ten pounds. It was difficult to believe that they were now a part of his family. There were tears in his eyes as he turned to his wife and put his arms around her waist.

"I cannot imagine what you have been through, Bess. You have made me so proud. This is my life now, here with you and our four children. We'll bring them up in Victoria, as I know you'll need the support of your mother and sisters."

The reunited couple heard a voice call out from the kitchen. They wandered down the passage, into the parlour and through to the small kitchen. Isobell's son Sandy was standing at the sink, his hands covered in blood.

He had just walked over from the abattoirs.

He was as tall as Edward, powerfully built with short light brown hair, and a freckled round face lit up by a warm smile.

"Don't come too close," he warned with a grin. "I've just brought some meat for mother. You can see, my work clothes are filthy and they're soaked with my sweat." Sandy looked at Edward and said, "So this is the missing husband. Elizabeth's brought a small battalion to live here and you are the man responsible."

Edward smiled back, "Well I hope I can solve that. I intend to buy a house as soon as possible. Your mother's been a wonderful support for Elizabeth and the children. I don't think she would have managed without your family's help."

Sandy was twenty. He had been working since he was fourteen, selling newspapers whilst jumping on and off the trams, and selling them to his regular customers at the railway station in the evenings. He'd also delivered groceries before finally getting permanent work at the abattoirs.

The young man had moved out of the house a few months ago to live with his girlfriend Judith in her mother's home, which was also in Burnley. Sandy had met Judith two years ago and she was now seven months pregnant to him.

Judith's mother was fond of Sandy. She was pleased to have a man in the house again, especially one who gave her so much help when she needed it. Her husband had been a soldier and was killed in 1917. She had two spare rooms and it meant that she was still close to her daughter. Judith was her only child, and she was also looking forward to the birth of her grandchild. Sandy had promised Judith they would marry after their baby was born and it was a big relief to Sandy to know there was a home for them with Judith's mother. He could not afford to rent on his pay of eight pounds a week.

Sandy spoke again to Edward, "If you're looking for a job it is easy to get one at the abattoirs, but you won't enjoy the work there."

The look on Edward's face confirmed that thought as he shook his head. "I can't bear the sight of cattle being slaughtered and all the cruelty that goes with it. I worked on a farm once and I care for animals. It would do me no good to try to work there as I wouldn't last a day."

The young man nodded. "Certainly my job this week has been tough for anyone to cope with. I've been collecting the hides after the cattle have been skinned, and stretching them out on the racks before they're sent to the tannery on the other side of Melbourne. Sometimes it takes a few days before the truck arrives. By that time they're infested with maggots. Apart from the stench, the maggots fall onto my shoulders and clothing as I lift them up on the truck. It's one job I hate, but I do get an extra pound a week for it. We rotate our jobs so I don't have to do it every week."

He sighed and continued, "It's time that we had some sort of Workers' Union for us. I know that things will have to improve. We have too many accidents there, and the pay is poor - but the bosses know there are so many unemployed men looking for work that they can easily hire other workers if we complain too much. I need this job because Judith is pregnant and I want regular work."

"Well," said Edward, "I couldn't do your job, for even an extra ten pounds a week."

As Sandy walked out the kitchen leading to the back lane he called out, "I'll come back later for dinner. Good to know you're back. My Aunty Elizabeth sure has missed you, and Mother will be pleased to see you again."

The front door opened and Elizabeth knew it was her sister Isobell's footsteps coming down the passage after finishing her job for the day at the weaving factory in Richmond.

Especially with the Depression affecting thousands of workers who could not find any other income but the 'susso', Isobell knew she was lucky to have a skill that was still wanted. It was because of her experience in Dunfermline weaving linen.

She was surprised to confront Edward in the parlour. "Och, Edward, you've arrived at last! And what a braw handsome man you are!"

Edward wrapped his strong arms around his sister-in-law and hugged her warmly.

"I can't thank you enough for taking such care of my family – you and your daughter, young Betty."

"Dinna fash yerself. We love the young laddie Trevor, and this wee lassie too."

Winifred knew she was being spoken about. She looked up at her aunty, and pushed away from her mother, allowing Isobell to bend over and put her arms around her.

"The tiny bairns take up most of Bess's time," Isobell explained. "She needs her man back here to take some of the burden from her. Your four wee-uns will be a big handful to manage for a long time yet."

Edward walked down the passage to the front room where Elizabeth, Trevor and the twins were sleeping each night. It had been the lounge, but now was terribly cramped, with a double bed, the two bassinets, Trevor's cot, and Elizabeth's sewing machine as well as a wardrobe and chest of drawers. Edward now would also occupy it.

Isobell and her husband Callum occupied the next bedroom, and Betty and Winifred were in the second small bedroom, which barely fitted in two single beds. The parlour off the kitchen was crowded with the lounge furniture as well as a dining table seating six. The kitchen was tiny and he imagined it would be almost unbearable to stand in it in the hot summer with the wood stove lit, cooking the dinner.

Edward walked into the back yard and saw the toilet backing onto the laneway. The home was unsewered and the laneway provided access for the pan man and his cart. Outside the kitchen there was a lean-to where the copper and concrete washing trough stood.

It was obvious that he would need to find a place for his family soon. Isobell was generous in allowing his family to stay and Elizabeth had needed extra hands to help her, but Edward saw how impossible it would be to live in such overcrowded conditions for much longer, especially in an unsewered area.

It was just before six o'clock when Elizabeth heard the cries of the twins. It was usual that when one woke the other one joined in sympathy.

"It is time for their feed, Edward. You might like to pick up Anne, and I will breast feed Isobell. I have nae enough milk for both, so they now alternate between breast and bottle."

Edward reached down and looked into the baby's eyes. His large hands were calloused and rough and he felt almost afraid to pick up Anne, as she looked so tiny and fragile. The little girl's eyes were open, curiously staring into this stranger's face. She had stopped crying and was content to be lifted up into his arms.

"Bess, they're perfect. What beautiful babies we have. You're a wonderful mother. I don't know how you managed to do it all. Your family has been amazing, giving you so much help. I promise we'll never be apart again."

Elizabeth handed Edward Anne's bottle and he could not take his eyes from her as she sucked greedily at the teat. The twins had short tufts of blonde hair, hazel eyes and silky smooth skin. Edward instantly felt such love for his new family and his eyes filled with tears. He could hardly believe how lucky he was to have Bess at his side and be blessed with such healthy twins.

It was after ten o'clock that night when Sandy finally left after dinner. He had shared two bottles of beer with Edward and was keen to hear about life as a cane farmer in Queensland. Winifred and Trevor were asleep, and the twins had finally fallen asleep after another feed.

Elizabeth looked pale and exhausted and was very quiet when they finally slipped into their bed. Edward held her close to him, putting his arm around her waist. She turned her head towards him. She could feel his erection harden against her and a mild panic set in.

"Edward, we canna risk having any more bairns. I spoke to my sister Janet, and her Tom is going to get some condoms for us. And you will have to use one - every time."

Edward kissed Elizabeth lightly. "Don't worry Bess, four beautiful children are enough for any man to help bring up. I've already bought some myself."

His wife sighed with relief as Edward said, "We have plenty of time to be together. Just having you beside me tonight is enough for now, and we might wake the twins if we disturb them."

Elizabeth was silently grateful for Edward's patience - she was so tired. It was also hot and she had not shared a bed with him for over a year. Making love could wait for another time. Very little breeze entered the room and Elizabeth felt hot and sticky with perspiration, and her breasts were sore. She thought it would not be long before she would need to stop breast-feeding altogether.

Edward also had not slept for twenty-four hours and he turned away from her. Before long Elizabeth heard a soft snoring as he fell into a deep sleep, just happy to have his wife by his side for now.

.o0o.

CHAPTER 34: Oakleigh

Two weeks had passed since Edward had returned from Queensland. For the first few days he was content to be with Elizabeth and the children, especially Winifred, who was still wary of this tall stranger who had appeared so unexpectedly, and was now sleeping in the same bed as her mother.

Edward made sure he gave Winifred plenty of attention. He took her to the park each morning with Trevor. Gradually she felt more at ease and safe with her father as he pushed her high on the swings and made sure that he was there to collect her at the bottom of the metal slide so she would not land on the hard earth. There was also the faint memory of a father who loved her, and her mother constantly reassured Winifred that this man was her real father who had come back to them.

Already Edward was desperate to find work. He could not afford to spend much more of his savings. The money was needed to purchase a home for them. Isobell was generous and very helpful to Elizabeth but the tenement was overcrowded, and their bedroom was stifling and airless at night, with the twins, Trevor and themselves squeezed into it with their belongings.

Four days after he had arrived the physical act of their lovemaking had woken Trevor and the twins. Elizabeth was tired and tense. It had been a year since they had joyously made love, but Edward was aware how uncomfortable Elizabeth felt. Her breasts were sore and he sensed it was an effort for her to pretend that it had been a spontaneous response to his urgent desire to make love to her again. He did use a condom and tried to be as loving and gentle as he could.

Elizabeth moved away from him saying, "I'm sorry Edward, I'm no ready yet. My nipples are so sore and I canna give masel' fully to you. The twins are still getting some of ma breast milk. I know it's been a year, but I need more time."

They then were awake for two hours, settling the children down again and feeding the twins. Edward realised that he had to give Elizabeth the chance to fully regain her strength, and eventually they would find that passion they had for each other again. They also needed their own bedroom free from the snuffling noises and crying of disturbed children.

Edward hated the area of lower Burnley near the Yarra River. The abattoir operated for twelve hours each day giving off a terrible stench, the constant bellowing of the cattle upset him, and the large local tip - a haven for rats, was almost opposite. How had his Bess coped, when she'd had such a horror of the cane rats of the north? It was essential that he move his family away from Burnley soon.

There was no friction between the two husbands in the household. Callum seemed to simply accept the presence of his wife's family in the house. Outside of his limited hours of work he spent much of his time at the neighbouring hotel, rather than confront his strong-willed sister-in-law. While Edward was less disapproving than his wife of Callum's evident slow descent into alcoholism – perhaps having a degree of sympathy for the frustration and despondency of being unable to provide adequately for a family – his whole focus was on his Bess and his own children, and doing the best he could for them. If anything, watching Callum's plight added urgency to Edward's search for work.

His farm skills were useless here. Edward was regarded as an unskilled labourer and there were hundreds of men like him looking for work. The Depression of the 1930's was still affecting many industries around Melbourne. Permanent work was almost impossible to find.

Edward had scoured the *Argus* newspaper each morning and had lined up with dozens of workers, but he did not manage to get one interview. He was almost prepared to take up Sandy's suggestion of a job at the abattoir, when he saw an advertisement for stokers to work at the Oakleigh gasworks. He knew nothing about coal stoking but this job would need strong fit men who could physically cope with working long hours in hot conditions. After living in North Queensland cutting cane, Edward knew he would have the strength and stamina to manage the long shifts and the heat near the furnaces.

The gasworks at Oakleigh were located near the train line and they were not too far from Burnley. Edward walked through the centre of the town and he was impressed with Oakleigh's size. The weatherboard bungalows were generally well kept with neat hedges and paling fences at the front of the properties. He spotted the large cylindrical gasometer as he turned the corner into Downing Street. It dominated the skyline across the area. There was a slightly foul sulphur smell coming from the gas works as he entered the gate.

In the gasworks office the manager introduced himself. "Welcome - I gather you saw the advertisement in the paper. My name is Jim Caldicott and I'm the supervisor here."

He was taken with Edward's powerful physical build as he stood before him and introduced himself. He noted Edward's thick muscled brown arms, his strong lean body and he was impressed by the honest answers given to his questions about Edward's work history.

"I can offer you a permanent job here, but I must warn you it's tough, physical labour for stokers. They work up to twelve hours shifts, including night shift work as the retorts produce gas continuously. Each one of them must shut down on a rotating basis, so that the waste product can be removed. I'll show you where you'll be working."

Edward followed the manager into the building and he was immediately hit with a blast of hot air and the strong smell of burning coal. Edward looked across at several workers shovelling coal into the retorts. Their faces were blackened with the coal dust, and they were wearing flannel singlets and heavy blue cotton trousers, or overalls.

"We need two sets of three workers at each retort. Coal is heated to a very high temperature to generate the gas, which is then siphoned off. Two men lift the point of the scoop into the retort and the third man pushes the coal in and turns it over. There is an unloading door at the back of the retort to take out the coke, which is what is left from the burnt coal. The gangs all work twelve hour shifts with quite a few breaks in between. They need to have 'smoko' time to drink plenty of fluids, and we have a canteen area for them."

One of the stokers turned to look directly at Edward and called out to him, "Ya comin' to work with our gang, cobber? We could do with a big strong fella like you. One of our gang has just left us."

Edward accepted Jim's offer of a start the following Monday. It was permanent work and he liked the thought of working with a gang of men again. He was not yet really aware of just how tough and demanding it would be, nor that the manager had had constant problems with his workers leaving after a couple of months because of the dangerous conditions.

Many of the gas workers suffered with terrible racking coughs, dying of lung diseases from inhaling the coal dust that swirled about them constantly as they shovelled. They sickened and died without any compensation being offered by the Management. It could be a few years after the stokers had left before their lungs gave out from being so damaged by the deadly black dust.

Edward walked back into the office, signed his employment form and asked about the weekly wage rate.

"The wage would be about eight pounds a week, with a chance of earning more with overtime. We operate on a forty-eight hour week, but most of the workers here work more than forty-eight hours and earn overtime pay."

Edward thought that the pay rate was fair, as he had spoken to other unskilled workers and they were earning about six pounds a week. However he had not yet experienced the dangerous tough working conditions at the gasworks. The manager did not mention how hard it was to retain his stokers for more much than a year.

During his interview Edward spoke to Jim Caldicott about renting or buying a house in Oakleigh, and the manager said, "Houses are cheap here. The banks own many properties around the area. Families have been evicted and their belongings put out onto the sidewalks. They couldn't keep up with their payments with husbands out of work. The Depression is still continuing and the factories are still not taking on many permanent workers yet. The banks would rather have houses empty, than have families living in them and not paying their mortgages."

After leaving the gasworks Edward wandered down to the end of the street and saw that it ended at the rail siding yards. He walked into the siding area and saw the coal hoppers loading coal onto trucks. The main rail line at Oakleigh continued on to the black coal mines in Gippsland and he realised that was why the gasworks were located up the street.

As he walked back he spotted a 'For Sale' sign on a small weatherboard bungalow not far from the rail siding. The bungalow was freshly painted with green trims around the window frames and it had a wide side entrance leading to the front door. Edward knocked on the door and was greeted by a lady aged in her mid fifties.

Edward introduced himself and said, "I saw the sign out on the fence and I was hoping you'd allow me to chat with you and take a look inside your home. I'll be working at the gasworks next week and I'm looking to buy a house near here that will be big enough for my family. My wife and I have four children sharing a rental and we're desperate to move into our own home."

The lady was impressed with Edward's openness and his polite quiet manner. She introduced herself as Katherine, and Edward was pleased when she invited him inside. He was unaware that there were four houses at the top end of the street for sale. Katherine and her husband had been trying to sell their home for over a year. Her husband had painted it four months ago to freshen up the exterior.

Edward entered the wide timbered passageway. Katherine showed him the two bedrooms opening off it. Then he looked into the bathroom at the end of the passage. A gas heater for hot water was over the bath, and the floor was covered in a thick green patterned lino. He entered a large room that was the lounge and dining area. The lounge room had two windows facing the side fence but there was plenty of light entering the room. He thought that Elizabeth could put her sewing machine there. She was anxious to start sewing clothes for Winifred and Trevor and herself, but there was no room for that where they were now living.

The kitchen was freshly painted with plenty of cupboards, and there was an enclosed wide veranda at the back of the house with a laundry and a sewered toilet. A small bedroom was at the other end of the veranda. There was a huge fig tree in the back yard, with plenty of space for a vegetable garden and a chicken shed against the back fence.

He smiled as he said, "This could be a fine home for my wife Elizabeth and our children. It's very handy for me to get to work, and I'll have plenty of time to help with the children."

He told Katherine about his baby twin girls, Winifred and young Trevor; the poor conditions they were living in and how he hated living so close to the abattoir and local tip.

"What a handful for your wife to manage!" exclaimed Katherine. "She will need plenty of help for a while yet, with such a young family."

Katherine invited Edward to have a cup of tea. She could see that he was impressed with the house, and hoped that her husband would agree to sell and move out as soon as possible.

She said, "We are keen to sell the house. We have lived here for twelve years and we intend moving to Carnegie. We have taken good care of it and it has been solidly built. All of the floors are hardwood. My husband put in the extra cupboards for me in the kitchen. My father died a few months ago and we intend living with my mother in her house. She is over eighty now, and struggling trying to manage the housework and shopping. My husband works for the Oakleigh Council and Carnegie is on the train line so he can easily get to work each day. We are asking four hundred and fifty pounds for this place."

Although Edward knew he could afford that amount, he also realised that he would need to buy furniture.

He said, "Would you consider an offer of four hundred and twenty pounds? I'm sure my wife will like your home, and there's plenty of space for my family here."

"I will need to discuss it with my husband tonight. You're welcome to come here at the weekend with your wife, as I am sure she would want to see the home. It is your wife who'll spend most of her time in it."

Edward could not wait to arrive back in Burnley and tell Elizabeth of his two strokes of good fortune. He walked into the kitchen, put his arms around her and kissed her on her mouth. He was bursting to tell her his good news.

"Bess, I have a permanent job and we may also have home of our own near my work! I'll take you with me and show you the home in Oakleigh on the weekend. The owner wants you to see it before we make up our mind. We can afford to buy it, as it's four hundred and fifty pounds, but we may get it for a little less if her husband agrees."

Elizabeth pushed herself away from his arms, saying, "I canna believe it, but I ken we must find somewhere to live soon. Our bedroom is so crowded and I'm so tired of getting up to the children. We canna make the slightest noise or we wake one of them. They need a room to themselves and so do we. I canna be close to you until we have our own bedroom. Isobell has been wonderfully generous but they need their space back. I ken that young Betty wants a bedroom to herself. Our lassie, Winifred takes up much of Betty's time. Betty is fond of our wee one, but says she keeps her from studying with her constant chatter."

It was just as well Elizabeth was ignorant of the type of work Edward had signed up to, or she may have changed her mind about their move to Oakleigh. She knew that Edward had loved farm life in Wales, and then working in the cane fields, and having his dream of owning his own cane farm. Knowing what he had agreed to do now may have tempted Elizabeth to move back with him to Queensland. But he never spoke of it to her. Edward was content to be with his Bess and his children. Nothing else mattered. He was determined to make sure he provided for his young family. He knew that Bess wished to be closer to her sisters and mother, and the train line from Oakleigh was convenient to Burnley.

A month later Edward and Elizabeth moved into their home in Downing Street.

Katherine and her husband had agreed to sell their home for the offer Edward had made. They also felt lucky to have met Edward who had the funds to purchase their home. Edward thought that the thirty pounds he had saved on the price of the property would buy the furniture they would need. With so many evictions, second hand furniture was selling cheaply at the auction house in Oakleigh.

However, Katherine sold them some of her furniture cheaply; a bulky thickly padded lounge suite, a double bed and wardrobe, dining table, ice chest and a wireless, which were all in good condition. Her mother's home was fully furnished so she was pleased to part with it. It was a new start for all of them.

.oOo.

CHAPTER 35: The War Years

Time seemed to have passed quickly for the Morgan family. It was two years since Elizabeth and Edward had moved into their small weatherboard bungalow. There were eight houses in the lower section of the street and two blocks of vacant land at the top of the street. One block had a small play area with two metal swings and a slide. A cross road separated the eight houses from the upper section of the street. The Council yards were opposite the eight homes, and the rail yards blocked off the end of it.

Elizabeth had settled well into her home. The house was big enough for the family and she had room for her sewing machine in the lounge to enjoy her tailoring. She made all of the children's clothes as well as her own. Her free time was mainly spent at the sewing machine, as often one of her sisters would supply material for a new dress.

Her sister Isobell often supplied woollen offcut material from the weaving factory for the children's dresses, skirts and overalls. Elizabeth was grateful for the fabric. She did not enquire too closely, but she was sure somehow Isobell managed to smuggle some of the material out of the factory, by wrapping it around her waist underneath her skirt. The tailoring skills Elizabeth had were well used, and the neighbours often admired the children because they were always well dressed.

Perhaps recalling his young days on a Welsh farm, Edward had purchased chickens and had planted out a small vegetable garden.

Elizabeth made several jars of fig jam as the mature fig tree was loaded with fruit each season. She had soon made friends with several of the neighbours, and as the chickens were producing about half a dozen eggs each day she was sometimes able to supply her new friends with fresh eggs. Elizabeth enjoyed her home, and the fact that Edward's work was so close, and so she saw him every day made it a very satisfactory move for her.

Edward's shift work meant that sex occurred much less frequently now, but in the privacy of their own bedroom they were free to enjoy their sex life to the fullest. Edward adored his Bess and, even though he was often exhausted after his shift, it was a delight to just wrap his arms around her and enjoy every inch of her body. Elizabeth would turn towards him, slide her hand down his chest, and lightly caress him. His weariness would be forgotten as their bodies came together with such passion. He knew when Elizabeth climaxed and it made their sex life complete and satisfying for both of them. Edward's heart overflowed with the emotion of his love for Bess before he collapsed into a deep sleep.

Australia had declared war in 1939 and it was now April 1942. The Japanese were rapidly advancing in the Pacific, and Australia's Curtin Government called up over 100,000 men to full time military service. This meant that there was a critical shortage of labour to keep up with the demands of the war effort. The employees at the gasworks were protected from compulsory enlistment, as gas production was declared a 'Reserved Occupation'. The labour controls were very strict, and were necessary to keep employees in essential industries. This meant that Edward was exempt from service in the armed forces.

During the War the Government had complete authority to say what every man should do, whether in the armed services, war industry or civilian industry. It had the power to prevent an employee from leaving their employment. It meant that Edward was compelled to stay working as a stoker, but it gave him security with his job.

For her part, Elizabeth was grateful that Edward would not be enlisting in the armed services. She could not bear the thought of him leaving her for years again, and she needed him here to help with their family.

Elizabeth had become very friendly with her next door neighbour, Barbara. Barbara had given Elizabeth a lot of help with the twins, particularly in their first year, helping her feed one of them whilst she managed the other one. The children now called her their Aunty Barbara, and they loved being with her. They would pop into her back yard and Barbara always welcomed them and made sure they were given a chocolate treat or sweet biscuit.

Her husband Ted had been called up in the army and had been posted to a base in Darwin, but he expected to serve somewhere on one of the Pacific Islands. He had written to Barbara saying there were rumours they would soon be posted there. The American conscripts were fighting in the Pacific, helping defend Australia, but most Australian soldiers were kept on the mainland or Australia's territories. It was likely that the Curtin Government would allow Australian conscripts to fight in the South West Pacific.

Prime Minister John Curtin needed Australian soldiers to fight the Japanese who were now a serious threat to Australia, and he was concerned Australia's war effort had to be expanded rapidly, if it was to be taken seriously by their allies. Ted was sent to the South Pacific in March 1943 and it would be nearly three years before Barbara saw him again.

Barbara was in her mid thirties, attractive, with short blond curly hair, and blue eyes. She had a sparkling, bubbly personality and a generous spirit.

An army supply base had been set up within the rail yard siding at the bottom of the street, and nine months after Ted had left, Elizabeth noticed an Army Major visiting Barbara's home. Her Army Major supplied Barbara with some luxury food items, chocolates, biscuits and nylons that were unattainable for most people during the war.

Privately Elizabeth was well aware of the 'payment' Barbara provided for the goods, but they did not talk about it. Barbara was lonely without her Ted, and the likelihood was that he would be gone for few years. After all, Elizabeth considered, she was much luckier than her friend. Edward was home most nights when not on shift work and she loved the warmth of his body beside her. Now that they had the peace of their bedroom, Elizabeth enjoyed all the passion they had shared in the early years of their marriage.

'Barbara's affair with her Major is her own business,' Elizabeth thought to herself. 'Why be critical of my friend? Barbara is getting pleasure and company from her handsome Major, who is probably married also. The poor lass probably would not see her Ted for three years. If she is enjoying companionship and pleasure in their sex life it is none of my business. Ted will probably never know about their friendship – certainly not from me, and I know that I cannot give my children chocolates with all this rationing.'

Elizabeth decided that she would never discuss Barbara's affair with Edward. He was fond of Barbara and appreciated her kindness towards the children and Elizabeth. Ted and Edward had often shared a beer together before he was called up in the army. She knew Edward would be hurt if he discovered Barbara was being unfaithful to Ted.

Rationing coupon books were introduced in 1942 for tea, butter, sugar, clothing and meat and Barbara often gave Elizabeth extra coupons. Often her butter or tea coupons were not enough to last the fortnight. Edward required plenty of sandwiches, tea and sugar to cope with the arduous twelve hour shifts and she always made sure her husband's tucker box was filled before he left for his shift work. Barbara cheered Elizabeth up whenever she entered her home with her chatter, and her extra coupons meant that she did not have to cut down on Edward's sandwiches.

Regardless of when his shift was to begin, Edward walked to the gas works. But before he came back to Elizabeth, he always made sure he showered at work. By the end of his time there his face would be blackened and his arms and overalls would be covered in coal dust. He did not want Elizabeth to discover much about the hot, dirty, dangerous conditions he was compelled to work under. He was prepared to put up with the stoking job because the pay was regular, and it meant he was close to his family. With Australia now at war, he knew he could rely on this job for several years as long as he stayed healthy, but that could not be taken for granted. Some of the men had developed racking coughs and he wondered when his turn would come.

Edward always had two days off each week because he worked twelve hours shifts, with extra overtime most weeks. He was then able to spend that time with the children, especially helping Elizabeth with the twins. He had missed a year out of the lives of Winifred and Trevor, and he enjoyed spending time with them, taking them to the swings and slide in the vacant paddock at the end of their street. He would spend an hour or two there, usually meeting some of the neighbours and their children.

Edward had been very patient with Winifred, as it had taken her a while to overcome her shyness and wariness towards him. He made sure Winifred got plenty of attention and love from him. She adored being with her Dad, being carried high on his shoulders to the park, helping him to plant seedlings in the garden, picking the vegetables, digging out the potatoes, and having him read her stories whilst tucked in her bed.

Trevor was just over a year old when Edward came back from Queensland. He enjoyed having this big gentle, loving man sharing the home. His mother had been so busy caring for the twins, Trevor had missed out on the special affection that he normally would have had from Elizabeth. That was unintentional, but almost impossible for his mother to avoid.

It was Edward who often picked him up when he fell, put him to bed at night when not on shift work, sang Welsh songs to him, and bathed him. Trevor loved collecting the eggs from the chicken pen that Edward had constructed, and occasionally chasing one of the chickens hoping to pick it up.

Life in the late thirties and early forties in the suburbs had certainty and security for the children. The mothers in the street worked at home, busy with all of the basics of life, cooking, sewing, washing and cleaning.

Elizabeth knew all of the neighbours in the eight houses, but it was her neighbour Barbara who she could rely on the most. Edward had cut a gate into the side fence through to Barbara's back garden and it was well used by the two women. The Morgan children visited their 'Aunty Barbara' often. Edward supplied her with plenty of vegetables from his garden, and had put up a rope swing on an overhanging branch of the large gum tree in her yard much to his children's delight.

The children were usually made welcome in most of the houses, and allowed to play in the back yards of the homes. The street was actually an informal network of mothers who looked out for their neighbours' children. The children could rely on their mothers being home to greet them when they came from school in the afternoon. Elizabeth and her neighbours felt comfortable borrowing small quantities of butter, sugar or other cooking needs occasionally, and sometimes lent each other small amounts of money for bread, ice or milk.

Pay rates were low in the forties, so that even to afford the block of ice, or buy milk at the end of the week caused anxiety at times. Elizabeth's neighbour Gwen came to Elizabeth asking for a shilling for the iceman at least once a month. Gwen would search everywhere, hoping to find the coin before having to borrow, but always made sure the shilling was paid back each payday.

Elizabeth did not pay rent, but three of her neighbours did, and their husbands were bringing home eight pounds week. It was a struggle to 'make ends meet' for them. No wonder that the vegetable garden and chickens were important in back yards then.

It was almost unheard of for women to divorce. It would create a big scandal, as adultery and cruelty were about the only 'acceptable' grounds for divorce. If any of the women suffered from physical abuse they did not talk about it.

Patrick and Mary O'Rourke lived two houses from Elizabeth, and often when she walked past their home, there would be loud shouting and swearing. She would see a dark bruise on Mrs O'Rourke's cheek when she came out on the street to buy bread or milk, but Mary O'Rourke never spoke to any of her neighbours about what had caused it.

She and her husband were Catholic and had six young children aged from four to twelve years old. It would be unthinkable for her to consider leaving. They were renting, and she was totally reliant on her husband's pay. It would also be impossible to find suitable housing for her large family, or ever find a job. Women in the nineteen forties were barred from many jobs once they married.

When Elizabeth had spare eggs she would knock on the O'Rourkes' door and hand them to Mary, but she was never invited inside. Often Elizabeth wished she could become friends with Mary and help her; perhaps sew some clothes for the children, but she was also wary of Mary's husband. He had grey unkempt hair, narrow lips, dark swarthy skin and his large stomach protruded over his grubby trousers. Elizabeth had seen him occasionally in the front garden but he had never acknowledged her brief greeting. She was sure he also would discourage any close friendships with his wife.

Elizabeth's strict Protestant background also gave her a prejudice against the Catholic religion. The three oldest of the six O'Rourke children were unruly, bullying and frightening some of the younger children when they were in the street.

If Elizabeth needed to shop, Barbara looked after Elizabeth's young family.

Everyone in the eight houses knew each other and apart from Mary O'Rourke who kept to herself, they looked out for one another. Elizabeth, like her neighbours, did not bother to lock her house. After all, what was worth stealing? The furniture in the homes was mainly second hand or large and bulky. Certainly there was little money left lying around and jewellery was the wedding or engagement ring, seldom removed from fingers.

The baker and milkman and iceman came down the street delivering bread, milk and ice by horse and enclosed carts. They were well aware of the low wages that men were being paid in the early forties. It was not often they needed to give change for a ten shilling or one pound note. It was copper pennies and small silver change of threepences, sixpences or a shilling that were handed to the tradesmen and vendors.

The mothers met out on the street as they purchased the goods. Only one of the households had a refrigerator, so the rest relied on the iceman to deliver the blocks of ice. He would carry it in to the home covered in a hessian bag and make sure it was cut to fit into the ice chest. There was often a race by the children to collect the occasional pile of manure that the horses dropped. It was a precious additive to the vegetable gardens of the families in their street.

In wartime, every little bit helped.

.o0o.

CHAPTER 36: Losing Tom

Elizabeth enjoyed visiting her sisters and mother in Burnley, especially Janet whose husband Tom had joined the army in 1939 because he could not get regular work. At least he now had a pay packet each week. Tom adored Janet, and it had been the most difficult decision he had ever made to leave his wife and children.

Janet longed to have Tom with her again sharing their bed and making love with him. The nights were the worst, as she constantly thought about him and often lay awake for hours wondering where he was, worrying when she would see him again.

In 1941 Tom was sent to the Middle East to join the allied forces as part of the British Commonwealth forces. Janet was unaware that Tom was fighting against the Germans near Tobruk until the dreaded telegram arrived informing her of his death.

She only found out that he was one of the 'Rats of Tobruk' who defended the port city so fiercely and bravely for months to stop the German advance, six months after he was killed.

It was a devastating tragedy for Janet, who was living with her mother Anne. Her daughter Fay was four and Ian, her son was two.

Anne was devastated when she heard the tragic news of her son-in-law's death. She had become very fond of Tom because she knew how much he adored her daughter and their two children. Tom had always been generous to Anne, spoiling her with occasional gifts of chocolates. They had shared many conversations and he understood how hard life had been in Dysart for Anne.

It was a blessing that Janet lived with her mother because she relied on Anne's emotional and practical support after Tom's death. The War Widow's Pension was meagre and meant that Janet soon was forced to return to her previous job as a tea lady in *Buckley & Nunn* in Melbourne. Anne, now seventy, became the carer for Ian and young Fay, walking them to the local school and cooking them the evening meals.

Elizabeth travelled to Burnley as often as she could, visiting her young sister and her mother and sewing most of the children's clothing. Her nephew provided meat from the Burnley abattoirs and his mother Isobell who lived close by in Burnley Street was a constant support for Janet and her children.

It saddened Elizabeth to think that the children would grow up never knowing their wonderful father, and she was determined that Fay and Ian would spend as much time as possible sharing holidays in the future with their cousins.

The Legacy Foundation was set up to help war widows after 1945 and gave Janet much help and funded the children's needs at school. They and others like them were called 'legacy children'.

In 1947 Janet met Chester, who was twenty years her senior. He courted Janet and flattered Anne with gifts of her favourite caramel toffees, chocolates and biscuits. Janet's sisters disliked Chester. They recognized that his desire for Janet was not reciprocated by their sister. She did not love him. However their mother Anne encouraged Janet to marry Chester.

She wanted her daughter to marry Chester, in spite of Janet's reluctance, to assure her and the children's futures.

"I ken that you'll never find another man like your Tom, my lassie, but Chester is very fond of you and he has told me that he will always look after you," Anne said.

He promised to purchase their rental home in Burnley and had also said that Janet's mother would remain with them for the rest of her life. Although Janet was not in love with Chester there were advantages because she would now have security for both her and her mother.

Ian and Fay intensely disliked their new stepfather. Chester had two children from a previous marriage who were now in their early twenties. He showed little interest in the welfare of Fay and Ian. He would occasionally discipline them with a leather strap, always checking that Janet was not there at that time. He would threaten them with more beatings ensuring that they were too frightened to tell their Mum about his cruelty.

For the children, this was the price of 'security'.

.o0o.

CHAPTER 37: Rosebud

Edward worked at the gas works in Oakleigh for several years. After the Oakleigh plant closed, he travelled across to the Boxhill plant, riding his bicycle up the steep hill on Warrigal Road. Gradually his physical strength weakened, and his skin colour changed from the golden bronze of his earlier years to a pallid grey complexion. He was still working over forty-eight hours a week. It was not till 1948 that an Act was passed by the Arbitration Court designating a forty hour working week, but by then, Elizabeth had made plans to save her husband's health.

Elizabeth became most concerned when he started coughing up dark phlegm. She knew that she had to get Edward away from Oakleigh, and the stoking job that would probably end up killing him. Two of his fellow workers had died and there was no compensation even offered. The Gas Company bosses were powerful, and it would need strong unions to fight for workers' rights. An individual worker was powerless against the management of the Company.

As Elizabeth's resentment grew over the mistreatment of the gas workers, she took much greater interest in politics in the 1940's. The 'May Day' march held every year to celebrate the granting of the 'eight hour day' was one way she could protest, and she would bring the children to sit on one of the Union floats. The march, with the solidarity of the Union movement behind it, was stimulating and gave Elizabeth hope for a better future and much improved conditions for ordinary workers.

She had never forgotten the terrible conditions in the mines in Scotland where her father was killed, and the suffering it caused her family when the mine management offered such a meagre compensation to her mother.

Edward and Elizabeth had discovered a cheap holiday camp for families at Rosebud in 1947. One of Edward's co-workers had gone there and found that cabins with shared community kitchen facilities could be rented for a pound a week. The holiday camp was close to the beach. The first time they rented two cabins, they were thrilled to find that Rosebud was like a country village. The water at the beach was shallow, and shops were close by. The children loved being able to walk to the beach with their cousins Fay and Ian, wander through the foreshore and mix with the other campers' children at the park.

It was on their second stay at Rosebud that Edward and Elizabeth purchased a block of land not far from the holiday camp for sixty pounds. Empty paddocks surrounded the block, and provision was made for a park reserve in front of it. They thought that they could put a cabin there and holiday every year at Rosebud.

Edward, however, was unaware of his wife's plan to not just holiday, but move to Rosebud and build a house on the block. She hoped that Edward would get a job locally and that he would regain most of his health. When they returned to Oakleigh Elizabeth contacted a Real Estate Agent.

"Ah dinna care what you sell this house for but I want us tae get two thousand pounds clear," she explained emphatically.

The house sold within two months. Edward moved to Rosebud, and three months later with the help of a local builder he had quickly constructed an unlined large cabin on the block and installed a five hundred gallon water tank. Elizabeth and the children moved into the cabin at the end of 1948.

Living conditions were primitive after the comfort of the home in Oakleigh. There was no sewerage, electricity or town water. For the children though, it was a great adventure. The beach was close by and they could explore it every day in the summer. Rabbits were everywhere, and to get to the local school was a walk through the bushland. They did not appreciate the hard work Elizabeth coped with - cooking, shopping, washing, cleaning the dirt out of the cabin each day, but she was determined that it was the best move to save Edward's health.

At weekends Edward commenced building their new home with the help of local tradesmen. A year later the family moved in to a home with electricity, town water, and a septic tank that had been sunk for a flushing toilet.

Edward managed to get a permanent job with the Postmaster General's linesmen, travelling with them each day repairing and maintaining the telephone lines all over the Southern Peninsula. He was with a gang of men again, enjoying the work in the fresh clean air. He had regular hours, with time to work in the garden. Gradually his skin regained its bronze colour.

There was plenty of space around the home with the park opposite, and empty paddocks where blocks were still unsold. Edward decided to buy a cow and tether it near the house. He had promised to one day own a cow again. He purchased a jersey cow and called her Dolly. She was in calf and before long Edward was supplying Elizabeth with rich creamy milk each day. There was enough cream for butter, and to supply their neighbour across the paddock.

He was totally content with his life at Rosebud and proud of his young family, watching them grow strong and healthy, living a life away from the temptations of the city, and having the strength and deep love of his Bess always at his side. Edward had long relinquished the dream of owning his own cane farm. He never did see his brother again.

His brother Llew had become a very wealthy cane farmer, but Edward did not envy him at all. Edward's wealth was within his generous heart, and in the enduring love for Elizabeth and his children.

Many times Edward had promised himself to return to Mackay for a brief visit with Elizabeth, and visit his brother Llewellyn but as the years slipped by his life was consumed with supporting his family. He rose at five o'clock to milk his jersey cow. He headed off to the depot on his bicycle, working as a linesman completing heavy physical tasks, digging and lifting huge poles into position for the telephone lines, often returning home exhausted in the evenings.

Compared to the horrific conditions at the gas works this life of rising in the early morning, putting his head against the soft flank of Dolly, smelling the scent of her rich milk, being home each evening with his family, especially to have Elizabeth lying beside him each night, curled against him with his arm under her soft breasts, gave him a great sense of peace and contentment.

Growing vegetables, planting plenty of fruit trees and enjoying seeing his children thrive in the healthy environment near the sea also fulfilled Edward's life more than he could have imagined.

Occasionally his work mates would drive across to Cape Schank and throw in a couple of lobster pots from the rocky shelves below the cliffs.

The salty spray rising up from the huge waves soaking Edward's overalls, and the sparkling freshness of the sea air made him feel so alive and invigorated in this amazing unpolluted environment.

As he regained his health his face and body recaptured their healthy golden colour and his physical strength returned. He knew it was because of Elizabeth's foresight and courage. It was his Bess who had insisted on selling their home, and was prepared to live in an unlined hut without electricity or sewerage till he could build their new home.

The lobsters that were hauled from the sea in the pots were large, and the men would take it in turns to share the catch. Edward would light a fire underneath a discarded copper in his back yard, boil the water, and watch the lobster shell turn a bright red. What a treat it was for his family, as he could never have afforded to buy one on his basic wage of eight pounds a week. Compared to suburban life, the daily 'cost of living' at Rosebud was much cheaper and healthier, and his family now could walk to the beach.

Every weekend for them was an adventure as they explored the countryside around them on their bicycles.

At weekends Edward often dug out septic pits to earn more money. The children kept ferrets as pets, and used them to catch plenty of rabbits. They would cover the entrances to the burrows with nets, and trap the rabbits as they fled from the sharp teeth of the ferrets. The open paddocks surrounding the house were covered with bracken ferns hiding dozens of burrows and in the early morning Edward would observe dozens of healthy rabbits nibbling on the fresh grass that grew around the cleared area of the block.

Fish were bought cheaply from the local fishermen, a large couta costing one shilling. Often Edward would kill and prepare a lamb for the farmer he had befriended where he had purchased Dolly, bringing home a half side of the tender fresh meat. They could never have afforded tender lamb previously.

Edward's early life in Wales on his Uncle's farm gave him all the skills he needed to supplement his wages.

Buckets of wild blackberries were picked every year for jam and as the garden was established vegetables, apricots, plums and apples grew in abundance. Edward kept a dozen chooks who benefited from the vegetable patch as well and provided plenty of eggs.

Elizabeth sewed clothes for all the family and there was plenty of cream and butter for cooking delicious sweet slices filled with apples, or a mix of spices and currants, or filled with jam with toppings of coconut. She was an excellent cook and she made sure her family always had plenty of delicious meaty stews of lamb, rabbit or cheap cuts of beef. On Sundays the Morgan children often invited friends to share in their mother's cooking and for some of the neighbours' children, the delicious sweet slices highlighted a memorable feast.

Elizabeth was well aware how poor some of her neighbours were, on their husbands' low wages, struggling to provide books and school uniforms for their children when they attended high school. She sent over enough milk each morning for her neighbour Mary, putting it in milk bottles so her children were unaware that it was fresh cow's milk and provided them with eggs.

Since settling in Rosebud Mary had become a good friend. Her husband was physically unwell but still struggled to work each day. His teeth were rotting, causing him considerable pain, but they could not afford the expensive dental treatment he needed. They had three sons and Mary was determined that they would attend high school and complete their education. Elizabeth sewed some dresses for Mary and altered and repaired jackets for her boys. Without her sewing skills Elizabeth knew she could not have afforded to keep her children clothed and in the correct school uniforms.

Over the years Edward and Llewellyn rarely wrote to each other, and eventually it was just an annual Christmas card that kept them connected to each other's family, with only a few details scribbled about their different lives. It was a surprise when Elizabeth handed Edward a letter from Mackay in mid April 1964. He did not recognise the handwriting on the front of the envelope.

Upon opening it and slowly reading the contents Edward looked across to Elizabeth with a shocked look on his face.

"Llewellyn has died. I never knew he'd been suffering from cancer for the past two years. He was just sixty three."

Elizabeth walked over and hugged Edward. She remembered how much he had loved his older brother and what help he had given them when they first moved to Mackay.

The letter had been written by Llewellyn's son Richard. It went on to say that two years previous, Richard's father and mother had visited their homeland Wales for the first time since his dad had migrated. Llewellyn had proudly told Meg's family of his success in Mackay, and he had arranged for new headstones to be placed on his parents and grandparent's graves in the Foel Valley in mid Wales where they had lived. Llewellyn owned three prosperous cane farms in the Mackay district and was a highly respected resident of the city, being on several committees there. He had no hesitation in telling the family of his prosperity in Queensland - a prosperity he had been told as a youth that he could never achieve.

The memories of his brother and their shared lives flooded back to Edward. He turned to Elizabeth and said, "I would like to visit Meg and her family. I'm sorry that I've let so many years pass and now I'll never see my brother again."

"Well, it is nearly thirty years since you last saw him. I dinna ken why you would go there now," was Elizabeth's first response, and then she saw the distress evident in his face. After a moment she continued, "Edward, it is too late now for Llewellyn, but not too late to visit the family."

Edward and Elizabeth did take the long journey by car three years later, and Meg made them very welcome. Llew's brother enjoyed seeing her family and touring around the prosperous cane farms, especially the one Meg lived in with its magnificent Queenslander home surrounded by tropical gardens, a mango orchard, and sugar cane stretching out to the hills. What a far cry from the one the brothers had worked on in the twenties.

Meg died in a tragic car accident in 1970, and Edward was thankful he had returned to Mackay and reunited with his sister-in-law and her family. Maybe, he thought, his family would eventually meet up with their Queensland cousins.

In her mid seventies Anne was diagnosed with serious diabetes. Maybe it was caused in part by the large quantities of sweets which Chester had plied her with. Anne was now considerably overweight. In 1952 Anne, now 80, was holidaying at Rosebud with Elizabeth when she suffered a massive stroke. Anne did not regain consciousness and died two days later.

Anne's children had always loved and respected their mother. Each one of them had their memories of the support she had given them in Scotland and in Australia. She would always have a special place in their hearts.

Perhaps it was the move to Rosebud in 1948 that extended Edward's life for another twenty years. Elizabeth was never fully informed of the cause of her beloved husband's death, but in her heart she felt it was due to all the years working in the gasworks, and the coal dust that damaged his lungs.

She would never forget standing outside the door of the hospital in Melbourne seeing her Edward coughing out streams of blood. His lungs had totally collapsed and he died within half an hour of her visit. She held his clean pyjamas and the sweet green grapes she had brought to the hospital for him. Elizabeth had the chance to see him before he died. It all happened so suddenly.

For months after that day her life stopped as she stayed at home, grieving so deeply for her Edward. It was the love of her children that gradually encouraged her to begin a life again without him.

.oOo.

EPILOGUE

It was April 1991. Elizabeth lay in her bed in the Nursing Home and her mind turned again to thoughts of her beloved Edward. Was it really over twenty years ago that he had died? She could not remember the exact date. Her deep grief and mourning at losing the only man she had ever loved had lasted for two years, but the memories of their life together had never faded.

They had raised their children at the beachside town of Rosebud where Edward had found permanent outdoor work. He had eventually built two homes and life was fulfilling, filled with the richness of their enduring love, raising their healthy children, encouraging and providing for them to be educated, growing most of their own food. He was content with his lot and envied no one.

Her life changed dramatically after his death. She moved away from Rosebud to live with her son Trevor and his wife, and then eventually come back to live with her twin daughter Isobell who had moved to Mornington Peninsula.

She looked up as her daughter Isobell walked into Elizabeth's bedroom in the Nursing Home and bent over to kiss her mother whose face still had soft pale skin with just a few brown blemishes, and whose thick, soft grey wavy hair was just falling below her ears.

'Yes,' Isobell thought, 'my mother is still beautiful with that generous mouth and those wide hazel eyes that glow with intelligence.' But it was her wonderful, strong, generous, personality that shone through and that still lit up her face whenever Isobell entered her room.

"What were you thinking about now, Mum?" Isobell asked.

What could Elizabeth say? A lifetime of scattered memories constantly rose into her mind. It had been three years since Elizabeth's first stroke. That had caused considerable memory loss initially, but much of her past had now slowly seeped back, and she was content to be where she was. Never had Elizabeth wanted to be a burden to her family, and at least here she was independent of all of them.

Isobell visited Elizabeth every afternoon and brought fresh fruit, occasionally homemade cake or an ice cream, and the talk was always about past memories, or interesting news of her own family or her grandchildren's lives.

It was late on Thursday and Elizabeth's thoughts turned back to 1928 when she had finally left Scotland for Melbourne. She remembered when she was ten and had recognized the poverty all around her in the coal mining villages, and had the strong urge to leave Scotland.

Elizabeth knew that her decision to break away from Scotland had given their four children and thirteen grandchildren opportunities that would never have been imagined when she first arrived in Melbourne. Edward and Elizabeth's journey had been rich in love, sometimes heartbreak, illness, and death, but it was a life well lived. Her grandchildren would have their own stories to tell in the future; but in coming to Australia she had given them enormous possibilities to reach whatever goals they wished to strive for, and enjoy the incredible benefits of living in this great country.

It was late Friday afternoon that Isobell received the phone call from the Nursing Home.

Elizabeth had suffered another serious stroke and she should come immediately. Her daughter Christine was now a practicing Doctor of Medicine and came into the Nursing Home with Isobell. Elizabeth looked up at the two women she loved, and had such a frightened look in her eyes. She held Isobell's hand, as Christine sat on the other side of the bed. Their presence was so comforting and reassuring. How proud Elizabeth was of her granddaughter as she listened to her calm voice.

"We are here with you Grandma, and we will stay beside you."

Elizabeth smiled up at Christine. She remembered her graduation, and the enormous pride she had to see her standing in her gown. Her thoughts had turned to Doctor Cowell and her admiration for his skills in the surgery. To now have a granddaughter become a doctor was overwhelming, when her parents had come from such humble beginnings in Scotland.

Shock forced Elizabeth's eyes wide open briefly as another violent stoke occurred, then she slipped into unconsciousness. Isobell and Christine knew that this was one that Elizabeth would never awaken from. They looked in deep sorrow at Elizabeth's closed eyes and their tears flowed freely.

It was just before midnight when Elizabeth stopped breathing. Her life had finished.

The two women walked away from the Home, but they knew Elizabeth would live on in their memories, and in the memories of her children for a long while yet. What stories they would tell of their amazing mother and grandmother who always strove with Edward to give her children and grandchildren the good life in Australia, the land Elizabeth called home.

.oOo.

ACKNOWLEDGEMENTS

I promised my mother Elizabeth that I would write a novel based on her life's journey. She died before I could complete my promise, and I have lived with that regret ever since.

Her story is now written, and it is deeply satisfying for me to have finally made that promise a reality.

I wish to thank my editor Henri Rennie for his empathy, for believing in my work, and giving me the courage to go forward with it through to publication.

A special "thank you" goes to my husband Stewart who gave me the time to write, taking on most household tasks and always giving positive but useful feedback when reading the drafts. His practical help was invaluable.

I would also like to thank my sister Anne, who has encouraged me and supported me along my own journey as a writer.

I have written this novel for the benefit of my extended family, and Elizabeth and Edward's descendants. I hope other readers will also find pleasure and interest in their story, and the story of their times. So much history is written about the 'prominent' people, yet all that they achieve is founded on the daily lives and experiences of the common folk, like those in this book. Those lives and experiences should not be forgotten.

Although the novel has been based on fact, it is a work of fiction. Many names have been changed to protect privacy, however the historical truth is just as my mother passed down to us – a vivid recollection of changing times and places.

ISOBELL McCONNELL
June 2019

www.ingramcontent.com/pod-product-compliance
Lightning Source LLC
Chambersburg PA
CBHW070533010526
44118CB00012B/1125